THEY COULDN'T BELIEVE THEIR EYES

"Then it seemed to tilt and come right at us. I automatically dropped to one knee and drew my service revolver, but I didn't shoot. I remember suddenly thinking that that would be unwise, so I yelled at Norman to run for the cruiser. He just froze in his tracks. I had to almost drag him back.

"The thing seemed to be about 100 feet up. It was bright red with a sort of halo effect. I thought we'd be burned alive, but it gave off no heat and I didn't hear any noise from it. I did hear the horses in a nearby barn neighing and kicking in their stalls, though. Even the dogs around the area started to howl. My brain kept telling me that this doesn't happen—but it was right in front of my eyes."

Bertrand's partner, patrolman Dave Hunt, arrived while the UFO was still in sight. The three stood watching in amazement for ten more minutes. "It floated, wobbled, and did things that no plane could do," Bertrand said. "Then it just darted away over the trees . . . "

Books in this series published by Berkley

The WORLD'S GREATEST UFO MYSTERIES

NIGEL BLUNDELL & ROGER BOAR

BERKLEY BOOKS, NEW YORK

Acknowledgements

The publishers wish to thank the following individuals and organizations for their kind permission to reproduce the photographs in this book:

Robert Estall 108 above and below; Mary Evans Picture Library 58, 95, 192 above right, (G. Lebat/Geos) 16–17; Fortean Picture Library 21, 30, 86, 135, 165, 192–193 below right, 198; Keystone Press Agency 7, 42 left, 90, 208–209; London Express News and Feature Service 66; NASA, Woodmansterne Ltd. 101, 214; Rex Features 26-27; Topham 37, 42, above and below right, 43, 107, 156, 206.

This Berkley book contains the complete text
of the original edition. It has been
completely reset in a typeface designed
for easy reading and was printed from new film.

THE WORLD'S GREATEST UFO MYSTERIES

A Berkley Book/published by arrangement with
Octopus Books

PRINTING HISTORY
Octopus Books edition published 1989
Berkley edition/December 1990

ISBN: 0-425-12498-3

Contents

Definitions

UNIDENTIFIED FLYING OBJECT:
Relates to any airborne object which by performance, aerodynamic characteristics, or unusual features does not conform to any presently known aircraft or missile type, or which cannot be identified as a familiar object—USAF Regulation 200-2.

CLOSE ENCOUNTERS OF THE . . .

First kind: Sighting a UFO in the immediate vicinity.
Second kind: A UFO leaves its mark, causes burns or paralysis to humans, frightens animals, interferes with car engines or TV and radio reception, leaves landing marks.
Third kind: Humans see or meet UFOnauts.
Dr. J.Allen Hyneck, Centre For UFO Studies, Evanston, Illinois.

Introduction

A president of the United States saw one, and launched a $20 million inquiry to find out more about it. The world's champion boxer saw one as he jogged in New York's Central Park. A Caribbean island leader saw one, and urged the United Nations to debate it. UN Secretary-General U Thant once called them "the most important problem facing the world next to the war in Vietnam." That war is long over, but unidentified flying objects are still being spotted.

Millions of responsible, reliable people have reported UFOs. Police, priests, politicians and pilots have all been astonished by strange craft performing inexplicable antics in the sky. A growing number of people claim they have actually met crewmen from these curious glowing shapes. Some have received injuries from the experience which have defied the best treatments that human medicine can devise. Some have even died from eerie encounters that proved too close. And despite the sceptical governments and scientists who say such things do not exist, UFOs have been—and are being—watched all over the world.

1

Encounters of the Worldwide Kind

For decades, people who claimed to have
seen unidentified flying objects were
derided and dismissed as gullible
buffoons. Yet UFO sightings continued to
pour in. Every year brings more evidence
from reliable witnesses of the highest
calibre. And their reports come from
every corner of the globe . . .

Year of the UFOs

Animals give the warning signals

Gary Flatter could not believe his eyes as he jammed on the brakes of his truck. Crossing the road in front of him was a curious menagerie of animals—seven rabbits, a raccoon, a possum and several cats. At the same time he was aware of a weird, high-pitched noise. The animals had emerged from a nearby field, and when Flatter glanced over the hedge, he soon found out why. Two silver-suited figures were staring at him.

It was October 22, 1973, and America was in the middle of a wave of UFO sightings. Flatter had accompanied his friend, Deputy Sheriff Ed Townsend, to State Road 26 near Hartford City, Indiana, where a car driver had reported two strange creatures standing on the highway. When they arrived, the highway was empty, and the sheriff decided to get back to town. But Flatter opted to stay on and look around.

When he turned a spotlight on the creatures, he saw that they were about four feet tall with egg-like heads that seemed to be covered by gas masks. Far from seeming upset by the light, they began putting on a show, jumping high into the air and floating down again. Then they flew off into the darkness, leaving a faint red trail.

Five days earlier, Paul Brown had seen two beings matching Flatter's description as he drove near Danielsville, Georgia. He told police that a bright light passed over his car with a swishing sound, and he saw a cone-shaped object land in the road some 300 feet ahead of him. He skidded to a halt, and as tiny figures emerged from the object, he grabbed his gun from the glove compartment, crouching behind the open driver's door ready to challenge them. They advanced no further, returned to their craft and quickly took off. Brown claimed he fired some shots at the disappearing UFO, but did not hit it.

Rex Snow ordered his dog to attack two silver-suited figures cavorting in his brightly-lit backyard at Goffstown, New Hampshire shortly after midnight on November 4 of that same year. The dog, a German shepherd trained to obey commands, bounded towards the intruders. But when she got within 30 feet of them, they curtailed their antics and just stared at her. She stopped in her tracks, growled at them, then slunk back past her surprised owner and lay down inside the house, whining and clearly frightened. Snow said later that he too was overcome by a sudden sense of fear. He had his 38-calibre pistol with him, but was shaking too much to hold it properly.

He quickly followed his dog inside the house, and watched the weird beings through the window. They seemed to be luminous, with over-sized pointed ears, dark egg-shaped recesses for eyes, and large pointed noses. Their heads were covered in Ku Klux Klan type hoods of the same colour as their suits.

The figures seemed to be picking things from the ground and putting them in a silver bag with slow, deliberate movements. After a time, they walked off towards some nearby woods. Snow rang the police, but before they arrived he saw the woods light up eerily, then become dark again.

Police were convinced that Snow had seen something odd and frightening. They said he was shaking like a leaf and still pale when he told them his story.

Three months earlier, on August 30, reliable witnesses in 22 towns in Georgia claimed they had seen strange craft in the sky. And on October 3, a deputy sheriff and four park rangers watched a saucer-shaped object "the size of a two-bedroom house" manoeuvre over Tupelo, Mississippi, the birthplace of Elvis Presley. They described it as having red, green, and yellow lights.

Dr. J. Allen Hynek, who established a Centre for UFO Studies at Granston, Illinois, collected 1,474 authenticated reports of UFOs during that year. Major-General John Samford, a former director of intelligence at the Pentagon, admitted: "Reports have come in from credible observers of relatively incredible things."

And Senator Barry Goldwater, formerly a major-general in the US Air Force Reserve, said: "I've never seen a UFO, but when air force pilots, navy pilots and airline pilots tell me they see something come up on their wing that wasn't a plane, I have to believe them."

A Gallup Poll at the end of 1973 showed that 15 million Americans believed they had seen a UFO—and 51 percent of the adult population believed that UFOs were "real."

Water diviners from space

Farmer Pat McGuire claims that 5,000 acres of his ranch near Laramie, Wyoming, were turned from dry sagebrush desert into fertile grassland because aliens on a UFO gave him a piece of good advice.

McGuire, his wife, eight children and a couple who live on his farm all say that unidentified flying objects of various shapes and sizes have hovered over their land almost every night for seven years.

"They are mostly about 300 feet wide and 60 feet high, and there seems no limit to how fast they can go," McGuire told reporters. "At first we were frightened by them, especially after we found mutilated cattle on the spread. One evening in 1976, my brother-in-law and I saw a craft hovering over a young calf. We heard the beast bawling for quite a while, then, when the UFO flew away, it took the calf with it."

The visits continued, but the herds were left untouched. McGuire and his family gradually lost their fear. Then, one night, the aliens made contact with the farmer, and took him aboard their craft.

He recalled the event under hypnosis administered by Dr. Leo Sprinkle, a para-psychologist with the University of Wyoming, and watched by an assistant psychiatrist.

In his trance, McGuire described the aliens as around six

feet tall, with large eyes, thin lips and bald heads. They told him to drill a well in high plains country, near his ranch.

McGuire consulted geologists and drilling experts a few days later. They told him the land was 7,000 feet above sea level, and he had no hope of finding water there. But McGuire went ahead regardless, even though neighbours called him crazy. He bought the land, bored his way through the upper crust—and struck a massive underground stream just 350 feet down. Soon 8,000 gallons of pure soft water were gushing from the desert every minute.

In 1980, after studying McGuire's claims both while he was conscious and under hypnosis, Dr. Sprinkle said: "I believe the craft appearing over his farm could be goodwill

---

The first flying saucer

Though unidentified flying objects have been reported above Earth for centuries, the first time they were described as flying saucers was on June 24, 1947. That was the day Kenneth Arnold, a fire-appliance salesman and an experienced pilot, took off from Chehalis Airport, Washington State, to help search for a C-46 Marine Transport plane that had crashed in the Cascade Mountains.

As he circled the area, looking for wreckage, a flash of light caught his eye. "I observed, far to my left and to the north, a formation of nine very bright objects coming from the vicinity of Mount Baker, flying very close to the mountain tops and travelling with tremendous speed," he said. "I could see no tails on them, and they flew like no aircraft I had ever seen before...like a saucer would if you skipped it across the water." Next morning, a newspaper coined the expression "flying saucer," and the Idaho businessman had his place in UFO history.

A US coast-guard photographer at Salem, Massachusetts air station noticed from the station photo-laboratory several brilliant lights in the sky. He grabbed a camera and recorded this sighting.

ambassadors of an alien civilization. I believe people like Pat McGuire are being chosen to spread the word that they are among us. And I believe we will see full-scale contact over the next decade or so.''

Visitors to the archery club

When two UFOs arrowed in on the Augusta Country Archery Club, Virginia, William Blackburn got the shock of his life.

Blackburn, who lived in nearby Waynesboro, was working alone at the club when he spotted two objects in the sky. He watched as the smaller of the two circled down to the ground, landing only 18 yards from where he was standing, open-mouthed with amazement.

Three extraordinary beings emerged from it, each three feet high, and wearing shiny suits the same color as their craft. One had an extremely long finger, and all possessed piercing eyes which "seemed to look through you."

The aliens advanced a few paces towards Blackburn. Although he had a double-edged axe in his hands, he was frozen with fright, unable to move. "They uttered some unintelligible sounds, then turned and went back to the ship, going in through a door which seemed to mould itself into the ship's shape," Blackburn said. "Then the ship flew up and disappeared."

Blackburn told UFO investigators that he had reported the incident to a government agency—he refused to say which one—and had been interrogated, then warned not to mention what he had seen to anyone.

Not in the curriculum

UFOs hover over school grounds

Brenda Maria's encounter with a UFO was almost too close for comfort. It happened in the grounds of the local high school in Beverly, Massachusetts.

At 9 P.M. on Friday, April 22, 1966, her neighbour's daughter, 11-year-old Nancy Modugno, burst into the room where her father was watching television, claiming that an oval, football-shaped object, the size of a big car, had just flown past her bedroom window, flashing green, blue, white and red lights.

When Brenda and another neighbour, Barbara Smith, arrived, Nancy was almost hysterical. Lights could still be seen flashing from the direction of the nearby school fields, but the two women, now joined by the girl's mother. Claire, suggested walking down there to put the child's mind at rest and prove that what she had seen was an aircraft.

On reaching the fields, however, they saw three brilliantly

lit, oval, plate-like objects flying in circles in the sky. One hovered over the school and building, the others were farther away. Suddenly, the nearest UFO began to move towards them. Claire and Barbara turned tail and ran, failing at first to realize that Brenda was not with them. Eventually, at the top of a rise, they turned to witness a terrifying sight. Brenda was screaming and covering her head with her hands, and the object was hovering only 20 feet above her.

"All I could see was a blurry atmosphere and bright lights flashing slowly round above my head," she recalled later. "I was very, very excited—not scared—very curious. But I was afraid it might crash on my head."

When the UFO soared back towards the school, the three women raced back to their homes to alert neighbours, several of whom also saw the objects. One called the police. Two officers arrived in a patrol car, and drove into the school grounds while HQ alerted the Air Force.

At the sound of two approaching planes and a helicopter, the three UFOs flew away. The neighbours were certain, from the lights and engine noises of the investigating planes, that the objects they had seen were no ordinary aircraft. For they had been completely silent—even when hovering right above Brenda Maria's head.

Communicating by numbers

Gary Storey's flashlight conversation

UFO enthusiast Gary Storey claims he exchanged messages with an unidentified object that flew past his brother-in-law's house in Newton, New Hampshire early on Thursday, July 27, 1967.

Storey had set up a telescope to observe the Moon when a bright glow had attracted his attention. Changing lenses, he focussed on it, and saw a series of lights flashing in sequence along the side of what seemed to be a large disc.

On impulse, Storey's brother-in-law flashed a torch three times. The object suddenly went into reverse without turning round. Then it dimmed its lights three times in answer to the torch.

The two men, both former radar operators in the armed services, could not believe their eyes. They flashed again, four times, then five. Each time the number was repeated by the disc, which was moving back and forth.

Suddenly they heard a jet approaching. "The object extinguished all its lights until the jet passed," Storey said. "We thought it had left. Then it reappeared, an oval-shaped white object, at least ten times brighter than it had been before."

The two-way flashlight conversation began again. The strange craft responded to one long and one short signal, repeating exactly the number and duration of every flashed message during nine or ten passes. Then it flashed all its lights once more, and vanished behind a line of trees.

Several scientists and UFO organizations investigated the claims of the two men, but none could find a conventional answer to the sighting. The local minister vouched for Storey's brother-in-law and his sister, saying both were God-fearing folk who would not lie or seek publicity. Their evidence was added to the dossier of sightings that suggest UFOs may be manned by intelligent beings keen to make contact with humans.

"Boomerang" swoops on factory

A friendly inspection from above

Workers on a repair gang at the Morenci copper-smelting plant in Arizona claim a massive spacecraft swooped on the factory in January 1981. It seemed to be examining one of the two 650-foot smokestacks by beaming a light ray down it.

The four men who were repairing the other stack said the UFO was shaped like a boomerang, and as big as four football fields. It had 12 small red lights on its surface, in addition to a large white searchlight beam underneath.

"It just sort of stopped in mid-air above the smokestack

and shone the big light right into it,'' said workman Randel Rogers, 20. His colleague Larry Mortensen added: ''I have never seen an airplane hover like that. I got the feeling that it wasn't aggressive. Certainly it did nothing to frighten us. Whoever was in it was friendly.''

A third member of the gang, Kent Davis, said that during examination of the stack, one of the red lights at the edge of the ''boomerang'' suddenly darted away from the craft at fantastic speed, returning after a few moments. The whole object then turned, without warning, and shot off like a rocket.

The UFO was also seen by 100 members of a high school marching band holding a practice session on the football field of Morenci High School, just over a mile away. Director Bruce Smith said: ''I looked up and saw all these lights in the shape of a V. There was no sound. It hovered for a few minutes, then disappeared high into the sky.''

Halos over the mission

The Papua sightings

Anglican priest Father William Melchior Gill finished dinner at his Boianai mission in Papua, New Guinea, and decided to take a stroll in the compound. He looked up to see Venus shining brightly. But what was that new light just above the planet?

As he stared upwards, he noticed more brilliantly-lit objects rising and falling through the increasing cloud cover, casting halos of light on the clouds in passing. Then he spotted something even more fascinating. Figures resembling humans emerged from one object and began moving about on it. There were two of them, then three, then four. They were doing something on the deck. Teachers, medical assistants and children came out to watch the strange activities several hundred feet above the ground. A total of 38 people spotted the figures over a three-hour spell before darkness fell.

Father Gill was a calm, painstaking and methodical man.

Alarm on the farm

A shiny silver saucer paid three visits to a farm at Cherry Creek, New York, on August 19, 1965. The four young farmhands who watched it turn clouds green and leave a red and yellow trail as it descended were not too perturbed, but the farm animals were clearly alarmed. A bull bent the iron bar to which he was tethered—and the milk yield of one cow slumped from two-and-a-half cans to just one.

He took careful notes of what had happened, and obtained signatures from 25 adult witnesses for his report. He dated it June 26, 1959.

The following night, the strange shapes returned. A native girl alerted Father Gill at 6.02, just as the sun was setting. There were still 15 minutes of good light left to observe four creatures moving around the deck of what seemed to be a "mother ship," while two smaller UFOs hovered, one overhead, the other in the distance beyond some hills.

"Two of the figures seemed to be doing something," Father Gill noted. "They were occasionally bending over and raising their arms as though adjusting or setting up something."

When one of the figures looked down, the priest stretched his arm to wave. He was astonished when it waved back. Another of the watchers waved both arms over his head. The two figures still on deck did likewise. Soon all four were on top of their craft, waving energetically.

One of the mission boys ran to collect a torch as darkness fell, and directed a series of Morse dashes towards the object. The figures could be seen waving back, "making motions like a pendulum, in a sideways direction." The UFO advanced for perhaps half a minute, and the group of witnesses—now about 12 strong—began shouting and beckoning for their visitors to land. There was no response.

"After a further two or three minutes, the figures apparently lost interest in us for they disappeared below deck," Father Gill said later.

The UFO stayed hovering over the mission for at least an hour, but later in the evening visibility became poor as low cloud moved in. Then, at 10:40, a tremendous explosion woke those at Boianai who had gone to bed. They rushed outside, but could see nothing in the sky.

Father Gill reported what he had seen to the Australian Air Attaché, who later contacted the US Air Force. The priest admitted that at one stage he thought the shapes "might just be a new device of the Americans." But the air force had no craft that could hover close enough for men

---

A hoax in the House

There was laughter in the British House of Commons when a Conservative MP quizzed the Air Ministry over a "flying saucer" which alarmed villagers in Lancashire in March, 1957. Mr. J. A. Leavey, who represented Heywood and Royton, demanded to know whether the Minister knew about "The Thing".

Parliamentary Under-Secretary Charles Orr-Ewing rose from the Government Front Bench and turned towards the Speaker. "This object did not emanate from outer space," he assured the House, "but from a laundry in Rochdale . . ."

When the guffaws had died down, he added: "It consisted of two small hydrogen balloons illuminated by a flashlight bulb and devised by a laundry mechanic." The man responsible for starting the scare in Wardle, a village near Rochdale, was Neil Robinson, 35. He said later: "I bought the balloons for fivepence each and sent them up as an experiment in tracing air currents. I never thought my little tests would be raised in Parliament."

to be seen on it, or could hover in silence. They had their own explanation—the sighting, they said, was "stars and planets." But as astronomer Dr. J. Allen Hynek wrote 15 years later after visiting the mission site, "I have yet to observe stars or planets appearing to descend through clouds to a height of 2,000 feet, illuminating the clouds as they did so."

Father Gill himself wrote a friend: "Last night we at Boianai experienced about four hours of UFO activity. There is no doubt whatever that they are handled by beings of some kind. At times it was absolutely breathtaking . . ."

There were nearly 60 separate sightings of UFOs over Papua that June. Trader Ernie Evernett gave what was probably the most vivid description. He saw a greenish object with a trail of white flame. "It hovered about 500 feet above me," he reported. "The light faded apart from four or five portholes below a band or ring round the middle of the craft, which were brightly illuminated. The object had the silhouette of a rugby ball."

Panic in the jungle

"All generators stopped . . ."

Battle-hardened American GIs in Vietnam grew used to the unexpected during the long years of jungle war. But on June 19, 1966, men at the 40,000-strong Nha Trang camp got the shock of their lives—and it came from the skies.

Hundreds of them were out of doors, watching movies on a newly-arrived projector, when suddenly a bright light appeared from nowhere. Sergeant Wayne Dalrymple described what happened next in a letter to his parents.

"At first we thought it was a flare, which are going off all the time, and then we found out that it wasn't. It was moving from real slow to real fast speeds. Some of the jet fighter pilots here said it looked to be about 25,000 feet up.

"Then the panic broke loose. It dropped right towards us and stopped dead still about 300 to 500 feet up. It made

Flight of the bubble bees

Three girl scouts from Malden, Massachusetts, saw a whole flight of UFOs in broad daylight on a camping holiday in August, 1965.

It happened as they were hurrying from their log cabin at East Derry, New Hampshire, to fetch water from a well after sighting storm clouds on the horizon. Dorothy Doone, 13, was the first to spot what she thought was an approaching group of low-flying aircraft, and pointed them out to her friend, Patricia Walton, 12, and her younger sister Shirley.

As they watched the "jets" get closer, their fascination turned to fright. There were nine objects, but none of them had wings, propellors or insignia.

"They looked like big, black overgrown bubbles with silver tails," the girls recalled. "Before we could run they passed right over the field next to us. They sounded like a swarm of bees. Then a big spark jumped between the last three objects."

Questioned first by their Scout leader—Dorothy's mother—and later by UFO investigators, the girls convincingly proved that they had not seen aircraft or helicopters.

this little valley and the mountains around look like it was the middle of the day. It lit everything up.

"Then it went up—and I mean up. It went straight up and completely out of sight in two or three seconds. What really shook everyone was that it stopped, or maybe it didn't, but anyway our generator stopped and everything was black, and at the air base about half a mile from here all generators stopped and two planes that were ready to take off, their engines stopped.

"There wasn't a car, truck, plane or anything that ran for about four minutes. There are eight big bulldozers cutting roads over the mountain and they stopped and their lights went out, too. A whole planeload of big shots from Washington got here next afternoon to investigate.''

Dalrymple checked out all six of the affected diesel-powered and independently operated generators for faults, but found none. Later it was discovered that a Shell oil tanker anchored offshore had also lost power at around the same time, for no apparent reason.

Captured on camera

Japanese photographers go into action

UFOs have been reported all over the Far East, and some have even been photographed. On October 10, 1975, Osamu Tsugaane snapped a picture of a golden shape that looked like a deep inverted pudding bowl over an air base at Hya Kuri. On March 7, 1973, Akiteru Takao spotted a silver globe over a suburb of Bangkok, Thailand, while on holiday there, and captured it with his camera. And on July 9 of the same year, police sergeant Yoshiyuki Matsuda took photographs of a traffic-accident scene on a corner in Nagai City—and revealed an oblong, egg-like glowing object in the sky which defied explanation by experts who studied it.

Hideichi Amano had no chance to take a picture of the frightening alien he met near Sayama City on October 3, 1978. Amano, a radio ham, had driven to a hilltop near the city to transmit messages without interference, leaving his two-year-old son asleep in the back seat. But when he returned to the vehicle, he found the boy bathed in an eerie light and foaming at the mouth.

The UFO below was photographed over the Iki Isles, Japan.

Please, Sir . . .

Twenty children aged six and seven dashed to the
study of headmaster Michael Yates at Wawne Primary School, Humberside, and told him they had
seen a strange object in the sky. The children had
never heard of flying saucers, but they described
a classic UFO—"like a dish upside down and with
a hump on the top."

He tried to start the car, but nothing happened. Then he
felt a metallic object being pressed against his forehead,
and looked round to see a creature with a round face, large
pointed ears, big, round blue eyes and no neck. The object
touching Amano's head was some kind of tube from the
being's mouth.

For five minutes, strange space messages were passed
telepathically through the tube into the man's mind; later
he repeated them under hypnosis. Then the alien simply
vanished, and everything Amano had switched on in his
panic—car ignition, lights, radio—burst into life.

The China syndrome

Sightings—ancient and modern

Chinese airmen and scientists have also spotted strange craft
in the sky. Though the government imposes a news blackout
on such incidents, reports of two sightings in recent years
have reached the West.

In July 1977, astronomer Zhang Zhousheng and several
colleagues at the Yunnan Observatory watched a glowing
object pass overhead, from north to west. "It was yellow
at the core with a giant spiral extension," Zhang was reported as saying. "It was very bright even in the moonlight,
and its colour was greenish-blue."

Ten months later, Air Force pilot Zhou Quington and other pilots were watching films outside their barracks in north-west China when a huge glowing object crossed the sky.

"It passed over our heads at 21,000 feet and disappeared behind some houses," Zhou said. "It seemed to have two large searching lights at the front and a bright tail-light. The lengths of the columns of light kept changing, creating a misty haze around the object."

Chinese history also records curious sightings. Shen Kua was a famous scientist and scholar who lived at Yangzhou, beside the Yangtze river, more than 900 years ago. He wrote of "a big pearl" that rose from marshes near the town, and hovered over a nearby lake. It had a round double shell and several people had seen it open. Inside was a bright, silvery light, the size of a fist, which dazzled anyone who looked at it. "All the trees around had their shadows cast to the ground," the scientist wrote. "The shell would leave suddenly, as though flying through the waves. It seemed to be surrounded by flame."

A cure for paralysis

A French doctor claims a UFO light-beam cured a paralysis that human specialists had been unable to treat. The doctor had been partly immobilized by a wound received in Algeria in 1958, and was also nursing a leg injured while gardening.

On November 2, 1968, he was wakened by the crying of his baby son, and hobbled to the kitchen to get him a drink of water. He saw lights flashing outside, and walked out onto the terrace to investigate. He saw two objects which merged into one before descending towards the house. A beam of light shone on him, then the UFO vanished as abruptly as the image on a television set that has just been turned off.

As he rushed to tell his wife what he had seen, he realized he was running—his wound, which had shown no improvement during months in hospital, had suddenly healed.

Death of the lavender plants

A French farmer said he was immobilized by two figures he disturbed beside a UFO in his lavender fields. It was July 1, 1965, when Monsieur M. Masse spotted a craft shaped like an egg and about the size of a car on his farm at Valensole, in the Basses Alpes region. As he approached stealthily through his vineyard, he saw two "boys" bending over lavender plants, and stepped forward to reprimand them.

He looked into the startled faces of two creatures unlike any he had ever seen. Both of the small "men" had a large head, long, slanting eyes, high puffy cheeks, a slit-like mouth and a long, jutting chin. One of the creatures pointed a stick at him, and he was unable to move. They watched him for a while, then floated up a beam of light into their craft. Its six legs turned, a central pivot began to throb, and the object floated upwards before vanishing.

It left a muddy hole in the bone-dry earth, and within days all the lavender plants close to the site had withered and died. New plants would not grow there for years.

Diplomatic incident

Portugal was plagued by a mysterious invasion of inexplicable flying objects during August and September, 1977. A senior British diplomat was one of many who reported sightings.

The alarms started when dozens of residents in the town of Viano do Castelo claimed they had seen a strange craft in the night sky. Then fishermen at the port of Portimao, familiar with the layout of stars, began to notice a curious intense light in a spot where no star usually shone. Finally, 12 firemen in the city of Guarda, returning from a call-out,

A UFO photographed at 4,000 feet by Shinichi Takeda of Fujisaw, Japan.

reported a mysterious shining object circling in the sky.

In September, the British official for the Algarve region, Mr. D. M. Armstrong, was alerted. An Englishwoman from the town of Alvor phoned to say that both she and her husband had heard a humming sound and seen an object hovering over their home.

The pro-consul fetched his binoculars and scanned the sky over Alvor, four miles away. He clearly saw an object flashing red, white and green lights, and estimated it was 25–30 degrees above the horizon.

In January, Mr. Armstrong wrote to Lord Clancarty, a UFO enthusiast in London, who had tried to instigate an official investigation into flying objects.

He reported his initial contact with the UFO, and added: "Subsequently, I was able to see at least one—and sometimes four—every night until mid-November, when we had bad weather, and have had almost continual cloud cover since."

"On one occasion I was watching two over the sea. I could see both in my field of vision when one moved suddenly and rapidly higher in the sky. I followed it and was interested to see, a few minutes later, that the second one had followed it.

"The effect is always the same, a rapid red-green-white flashing around what would appear to be a circular base. I have seen nothing by day, only in the evening."

The diplomat added: "As you may imagine, I received derision from my acquaintances, but when people came to dinner I would mention the fact and then take them into the garden with my glasses. Everyone had to admit there was 'something unusual' there. The derision ceased at once."

The Portuguese Embassy in London was unable to throw any light on the sightings. But it then admitted to an "incident" involving a Portuguese airliner. The pilot had radioed that he was being buzzed by a circling object that was nothing like any aircraft he had ever seen.

"Cigar" over the Seine

Unidentified Flying Objects of different sizes operating together were reported from the small French town of Vernon in the early hours of August 23, 1954. Businessman Bernard Miserey had just parked his car in his garage at 1 A.M. when he spotted a huge, long, silent, luminous cigar-shaped object suspended over the river Seine, 300 yards from where he stood. It cast an eerie glow over the dark houses of the town.

M. Miserey watched for several minutes. "Suddenly from the bottom of the cigar came an object like a horizontal disc," he recalled. "It dropped in free-fall, then slowed, swayed, and dived horizontally across the river towards me, becoming much brighter, surrounded by a halo. A few minutes after it disappeared behind me, going southwest at a prodigious speed, a similar object came from the cigar and went through the same manoeuvres.''

Five discs in all fell from the cigar, and shot off in different directions. After the last emerged, the cigar faded into darkness. M. Miserey went next morning to tell the police what he had seen—and was informed that two policemen and an army engineer had seen exactly the same thing, at the same time.

Out among the berries

Two Norwegian sisters told police they spoke to a man from a flying saucer in August 1954. The women, aged 32 and 24, said they were picking berries in the hills near Mosjöen, in central Norway, when a dark, long-haired man in a buttonless khaki outfit motioned them into a hollow. In it they saw a saucer-shaped craft about 16 feet wide.

The man tried to communicate with words, gestures, and drawings. But the sisters could not understand him, and he showed no signs of comprehension when they spoke to him in French, German and English.

Finally the stranger climbed back into the saucer, which rose fast into the air with a humming sound, like a swarm of bees.

Army manoeuvres

Two British soldiers say they saw a UFO while on exercises with the Royal Armoured Corps in 1978. Mike Perrin and Titch Carvell were driving their Land-Rover on the Yorkshire moors when they saw a dome-shaped silvery object hovering 50 yards away, making a strange buzzing sound.

A Scottish saucer

Two ten-year-old girls at Elgin, north-east Scotland, described "a silver-coloured saucer with a bump on the top" which they had seen hovering in a wood. The craft glowed with a red light and a silver-suited man stood beside it. Mrs. Caroline McLennan, mother of one of the girls, said: "When my daughter told me about it, I remembered having heard a strange whirring noise and saying to my neighbour, 'Sounds like a flying saucer.' The girls led us back to the wood and we found a big patch of flattened grass. The leaves on the trees nearby were scorched."

"It was about the size of five Land-Rovers and had portholes," said Perrin, 27. "Lights inside were flashing red and white. I tried to start our vehicle, but the engine was totally dead. We watched the UFO for five minutes, then it shot off and all the power returned to our engine."

He added: "It's army policy to dismiss UFO reports, but when we went back to the area next morning with a sergeant, we found a large circle of burnt grass where the object had hovered."

"Draw what you saw..."

When netball teacher Bronwen Williams spotted a strange object in the sky during a game she was supervising in February 1977, she knew exactly what to do. She ushered her nine pupils inside Rhos-y-Bol county primary school at Anglesey, gave them pencils and paper, and told them to draw, without conferring, what they had seen. The pictures tallied remarkably—a cigar-shape with a black dome.

That same night policeman's wife Hilda Owen was looking out of her kitchen window when she too noticed a shape gliding silently in and out of the clouds. She drew it in lipstick on the window glass, and her husband made a copy on paper when he returned from duty. It might have been drawn by one of the schoolgirls.

Mrs. Owen said the UFO appeared from a "a tongue of flame" over Aberffraw Common. "At first I thought an aircraft was on fire, but within seconds the flame appeared to form a circle and a domed figure appeared," she said. "There was no mistaking the shape. I could see portholes quite clearly."

The shape was still in the sky when her husband arrived home just after midnight. "It was the colour of the setting sun and about twice the size of the sun as we see it," he said. "By the time I got my binoculars out, it had vanished."

The hole in the hedge

"I was cold and terrified . . ."

Nine-year-old Gaynor Sunderland dashed home breathless and too scared to speak one day in July 1976. Her mother Marion calmed and comforted her, then listened to her description of what was later described as "probably the best UFO encounter ever documented in Britain."

Gaynor had seen a strange, silver, saucer-shaped object land in a field a mile from her home in Oakenholt, near Flint, North Wales. She lay quietly, terrified but fascinated, peering through a gap in a hedge. Two silver-suited people emerged from the craft and probed the ground with equipment. They were short and angular with large pink eyes, and seemed to be a man and a woman.

The craft they came from was around 35 feet long and nine feet high. It had a band of yellow windows along the side, and a flashing box on the top. There was a loud humming noise when it took off again after about half-an-hour.

Gaynor told her mum: "I was cold and terrified—I was sure both of them had seen me." But for 18 months, her

This UFO was photographed over Lago Maggiore near the little town of Arona, Italy at 10:30 P.M.. on March 3, 1979. The event was wit-

nessed by many and the photograph was published in local newspapers.

story remained a family affair. Mrs. Sunderland explained: "Gaynor was frightened of ridicule." At last the child plucked up the courage to tell others. She was twice questioned under hypnosis, and produced drawings of what she had seen.

UFO watcher Jenny Randles, of *Flying Saucer Review,* said: "Gaynor's description is among the most detailed ever recorded."

The clicking "dolls"

Three women in northern England claim to have seen white, doll-like aliens emerge from UFOs. All reported their experience to researchers, but insisted on remaining anonymous.

The first encounter came in September 1976. Two women, aged 63 and 18, were walking near their homes at Fencehouses, Tyne and Wear, when they saw a small, oval object, and found themselves hypnotically attracted by it. As they approached, two beings, "the size of large dolls," appeared. They had large round eyes and white hair. They seemed startled, and retreated quickly.

Exactly three years later, a 23-year-old woman was in her bedroom at Felling, Tyne and Wear, at 4 A.M. when a glowing, glittering bell-like disc actually entered the room. "There was a buzzing noise everywhere and I felt paralyzed," the woman told investigators. "Then 12 white creatures appeared, small, like dolls. They were making clicking noises and seemed to be watching me. One even touched me. Then they disappeared."

UFO researcher and author Jenny Randles said: "I am convinced the women are telling the truth about genuine experiences. In one way the reluctance of the witnesses to get involved lends credence to their stories. At least we know they are not after cheap publicity."

At nearby Killingworth, a 21-year-old nurse who would agree only to be identified as Linda, reported a UFO flying between two houses in February 1978. There was a deafening build-up of sound, and her mother hid under the bedclothes, convinced a plane was about to crash. But Linda looked out of the window, and saw, only feet away, a silvery object with a string of coloured lights. She said it looked "like a tin containing expensive cigars."

Weird happenings in the South West

A courting couple, a builder's wife and a deck-chair attendant all saw something strange in the sky on the night of Saturday, May 21, 1977. All the sightings were near Poole, Dorset.

Pretty 18-year old tax officer Karen Iveson and her boyfriend, apprentice technician Cliff Rowe, 19, had just parked their car on a lonely road near Parley Cross when a beam of light struck the back of it.

"We couldn't see what was causing it, but it scared us a little, so we decided to move on," said Cliff. Back on the road, they saw what had disturbed them.

Karen said: "A large, silvery disc-shaped object hovered over a field, and a silver-green, cone-like beam of light shone down from the centre of it. We stopped to watch, and it seemed to stay there for ages. Then it suddenly veered off fast and dropped behind some trees, much lower than any plane could go. We both panicked afterwards. It was not like anything I'd ever seen before."

Builder's wife Pauline Fall, 31, saw the same thing only miles away as she drove down a dark country lane near the village of Longham. A beam of light fell across the car bonnet four or five times, "as if something was tracking us," but at first Pauline could not see where it came from.

"One minute there was nothing in the sky, the next there it was, looking like the underside of a big dinner plate," she recalled. Out of the centre came a silvery white light, narrow at the top and widening into a cone. It was solid light, as if a line had been drawn round it.

"I'm not normally one to panic, but the pit of my stomach went ice-cold. A friend with me was unnerved, too."

STRANGE OBJECTS
HAVE BEEN SIGHTED
IN THE
SHEFFIELD SKIES

- The Air Ministry cannot explain them

- This picture has been analysed by experts. It is genuine, they say

- **WE SAY:** How much longer dare we pooh-pooh stories such as these?

These UFOs were sighted and photographed over Conisbrough, South Yorkshire, England on March 28, 1966.

Pauline kept driving for home, even though the beam seemed to be getting shorter as the object descended. "Then it just disappeared as if it had been swallowed up by the ground."

When Pauline got home to Wimborne, husband John thought from the look of terror on her face that she must have had an accident. Her hands were as cold as ice, and it was an hour before warmth began to creep back into them.

Odd things happened to Pauline's car after that night. Petrol consumption shot up, and the engine, perfectly all right when John was at the wheel, inexplicably cut out when Pauline was driving. She refused to take it out alone at night for four months.

"I've done a lot of soul-searching, but I haven't found a logical explanation for what I saw," Pauline said. "I just wish someone could tell me what it was, where it came from, and what it wants from us."

The third person to see the craft was deck-chair attendant Richard Morse, 27, who spotted a flickering light behind clouds as he hurried to a bus in Poole. "I thought it was the Moon, then I saw the Moon in another part of the sky.

"Just looking at it made me feel weird. It was a flying saucer shape with another shape on top and a beam of white light from its centre to the ground. Time seemed to stand still as I watched, then the thing started to move off, banking very fast, before it disappeared. It wasn't like anything from this planet . . . I was really glad to hear others had had similar experiences that night, because my friends were starting to think I was mad!"

Along the coast at Parkstone Dorset, Mrs. Ethel Field had a strange encounter in March, 1978, when she left her husband and daughter watching television to bring in washing from her back garden.

"Suddenly I saw this object in the distance, rising from the sea," she said. "It ascended and came closer. It was circular with a dome on the top. Beneath it were several lights, shielded by hoods that looked like eyelids. When the lids slid back, there were spotlights lighting the ground.

"I was frightened and stunned. It hovered directly above

me. The lights were so strong that I put my hands up to screen my eyes.

"Then I saw two figures standing in front of an oblong window. They had longish faces and were wearing silver suits and what looked like skull caps. They seemed to be standing at some controls.

"I felt that some power was holding me where I stood. I waited, shielding my eyes. Then one of the figures turned away from me to look at his companion. The minute he did that, I felt a release and ran petrified to call my husband and daughter. They laughed at me and wouldn't leave the TV."

Mrs. Field spent several sleepless nights worrying about what she had seen. Then red blotches appeared on the hands that the light had hit. Soon her hands were raw, with skin flaking and scaling all over them. "I went to several doctors about it, but only one listened seriously to what I told him," she said.

Backwards in time

Salesman Alan Cave, 45, of Taunton, Somerset, remembers the precise moment he became a "time traveller." As he was driving, one October morning in 1981, from Bath to Stroud, his car passed directly beneath a strange, orange, cloud-like object in the sky.

"I know it was exactly 11 o'clock," said Alan, "because a newsreader announced the headlines on the car radio. But then I glanced at my watch and it said 8 o'clock. My digital pen said 9. Both were right when I set out.

"Then the speedo started going back—it was weird. It lost 300 miles, though a mechanic has since told me it was impossible."

Alan doesn't believe in flying saucers, "but something very odd occurred in those few seconds and I wouldn't like it to happen again."

The British Flying Saucer Research Bureau later said they investigated several reports of a UFO in the same area. They added that checks on aircraft movements had not provided an explanation.

Scary New Year

Weird sightings were reported throughout Britain on New Year's Eve, 1978. Schoolboy Andrew McDonald, 13, claimed he was buzzed by a UFO as he rode his bike home through Runcorn, Cheshire.

"I heard a hum like a high-pitched engine" said Andrew. "I looked up and there was a big white light with a very bright trail above me. It stayed with me for about ten seconds, then soared up into the sky. I could feel it trying to lift me off the ground." Andrew was so unnerved that he could not cycle any farther.

In London, nightclub waitress Patricia White saw a blazing white shape as a taxi drove her home through Wembley. "It shone like a big, bright star, but it was following the cab," said Mrs. White, 34, of Harrow. "I was petrified, and so was the cab-driver."

Scared witnesses also reported seeing unexpected lights and shapes above Newcastle upon Tyne, Sheffield, Manchester, Norwich, and places in Scotland. But the Ministry of Defense said: "We are not being invaded. We think it is just some space debris burning up."

Marooned on the moors

A good turn proved a nightmare for Lillian Middleton. She drove out onto the lonely Northumberland moors to rescue a friend who was stranded—and ended up being chased for miles by a terrifying UFO.

The ordeal began at 2:30 A.M. on August 21, 1980, when the bedside phone rang at Mrs. Middleton's home in Seaton Delaval, Whitley Bay. The 33-year-old woman agreed to drive out to her friend, whose car had run out of petrol. But as she reached the moors, she saw a bright flash of light.

"I thought a plane had caught fire or exploded in mid-air," she said later. "I slowed down and peered out of the window. I was shocked to see a huge rugby ball shape giving off a brilliant light and hovering in the sky. It suddenly zoomed down towards me. I was terrified.

"It seemed about the size of two big cars. I put my foot down and was soon doing 70 mph in an effort to get away, but the thing kept with me, hovering just above the roof. It moved to the side from time to time, as if it was trying to see who was inside. After what seemed an eternity, I saw my friend beside his car. He too had seen the shape."

The UFO followed them all the way to the petrol station, a few miles away. A taxi driver and a couple in another car had also watched it approaching. Armed with a can of petrol, Mrs. Middleton set out again for the stranded car.

"This time the UFO zoomed right down low to car roof-top height," she recalled. "My friend became as scared as I was, and we turned round and went back to the service station. I wasn't going down that lonely road again. I cried with relief that someone else had seen what had happened. The other couple were still at the garage, and we all watched the thing for some time until it suddenly shot off at speed and disappeared."

Mrs. Middleton rang the police, who were sympathetic. Indeed, their own chief inspector had also reported seeing the UFO. But the experience left its mark. "I was in a state of shock for several weeks," Mrs. Middleton said. "Now I won't go out driving after dark, and for a long while I couldn't bring myself to look into the night sky."

Aliens over Russia

For years, the Kremlin authorities mirrored the attitude of air chiefs in America—UFOs did not exist. Sightings were dismissed as cloud formations, planets and the like, or fobbed off with some other logical explanation; and people who reported strange craft were considered idiots who also believed in goblins and fairies.

But in the late 1970s, *Pravda* began publishing accounts of mysterious visitors all over the country. And they were every bit as astonishing as those reported in the West.

Dr. V. G. Paltsev, a veterinary surgeon, was making his country rounds, 500 miles from Moscow, when he came across a grounded craft. Three small humanoids with egg-shaped heads and long fingers were standing beside it, but as he approached them, he was knocked out by a strange force.

He came round to find his watch had stopped. Above him, a glowing saucer shape was disappearing. Dr. Platsev went home, and carried on working as if nothing had happened. But at night, he repeatedly dreamed that he had been carried onto the craft while unconscious.

A doctor interrogated him under hypnosis—and decided that the vet probably had been taken for a ride on the saucer.

Dr. A. I. Nikolaev, a respected historical sciences professor, spent three months in hospital recovering from his close encounter. He and three academic colleagues were on a camping holiday in southern Russia when they came across a metallic, saucer-shaped craft partly hidden in long grass. One of them threw some stones, which seemed to disappear inside the object.

All four men then felt a strange force. Dr. Nikolaev was knocked out. The others, though drowsy, dragged him away. Two stayed with him while the third went for help: but both sentries soon fell asleep.

When they woke, two three-foot figures in space suits and helmets were staring at them. At the first signs of life, the small humanoids scurried back to their craft, vanishing from sight through the hull. The object glowed, then disappeared.

Professor F. Zigel, who led the official team of investigators into the case, said: "There is no doubt that a spaceship landed—possibly because of illness among the crew."

Only days later, three other scientists saw an alien craft just 67 miles from Moscow. They too were camping, and that night in their tents they heard a babble of loud voices. None of them recognized the language, but all felt a sense of unaccountable fear.

It was half-an-hour before they dared look outside—and there stood a shining violet-coloured object, about 80 feet high, looking "something like a giant electric light bulb." It rose, swayed slightly, then soared upwards into a fluorescent cloud.

Next morning, the campers found a circle of flattened grass 500 feet from their tents . . . and called in the investigators.

The Russians showed unexpected interest in an English UFO sighting. Hope and Ruby Alexander spotted a bright, triangular light hovering over Hayes Road, Bromley, Kent, as they drove home one evening in 1978 after a concert. Their sighting was reported in the local newspaper, which noted that there seemed no explanation for it. The two women preferred to let the subject drop.

But two years later, the paper received a postcard from the Soviet science city of Novosibirsk. Someone signing himself V.I. Sanarov asked for a copy of the article, and any further information available. Hope said: "We were astonished at the interest after all this time."

Charles Bowen, editor of the British magazine *Flying Saucer Review*, said: "Soviet scientists have a great interest in UFOs. For several years the Soviet Academy of Science has been ordering three copies of every issue of the *Review*, and last year I had half a dozen letters from people in the Soviet Union asking for information on the subject."

The Bermuda riddle

Dozens of ships have disappeared in the Bermuda Triangle since the US Navy craft *Cyclops* sank with 300 men in 1918. Aircraft, too, have vanished without trace, including five Avenger bombers from Fort Lauderdale that reported having lost their bearings on a routine flight in 1945, and were never seen again. But in 1978 it was a mystery arrival

The US Navy supplyship *Cyclops* vanished with 300 on board on March 4, 1918. The speed of its disappearance is witnessed by the fact that the ship's officers had no time to wireless a distress signal.

which baffled the experts who keep watch on the area of sea between Florida, Puerto Rico and Bermuda.

Radar crews at the Pinecastle Electronic Warfare Range near Astor, Florida, suddenly found a zig-zagging shape on their screens at a time when no military or civilian planes were expected. And it quickly became clear that this was no ordinary plane. The object was moving in a very erratic way, changing direction at incredible speed, suddenly stopping, then accelerating, within seconds, to 500 mph. Officers scanned the skyline with binoculars, and saw a circular craft emitting curious red, green and white lights. Nobody knew what it could be.

"It manoeuvered in such a way and at such speeds that it could not have been an airplane or helicopter," said one technician. "I've never seen anything like it—and I don't want to see anything like it again."

At 5:30 A.M. on September 27, 1979, two children on the island of Bermuda claimed they were immobilized by strange noises from a UFO. Laquita Dyer, 13, and her brother Melvin, 11, were sleeping in separate rooms when both heard a loud, rasping, buzzing sound coming from above their roof.

"When I tried to get up, I couldn't move at all, I was paralyzed," said Melvin. His sister said: "I tried to get to the window, but couldn't." After about ten minutes, the noise switched to a softer tone, then stopped. Only when it died away could the children move their limbs again.

The children's ordeal came only hours after many other people reported a UFO streaking across the sky to the south of the island. Jeffry Schutz, a consultant with the US Department of Energy, was one of them. He was with his mother and sister on the patio of his home. "At about 9:45 P.M. we saw an object travelling from west to east, climbing at an angle of 45 degrees," he said. His sister Betsy, 23, said: "It was a yellowish, whitish ball, faster than a satellite but slower than a shooting star. It was climbing in a clear sky, with a white vapour trail. We watched it for 20 seconds, then it vanished with a greenish glow."

English teacher Nigel Kermode and his wife Julie also saw the UFO from their porch. He said: "It was much too bright and big to be an airplane." She said: "It seemed to lose momentum and then speed up again. Then it just disappeared."

Local tracking stations had no explanation for the sightings.

The green-suited Superman

A strange flying humanoid dropped in on a family in Puerto Rico on July 12, 1977, according to a man who lived in the town of Quebradillas. He said he and his daughter were at home that day when a small figure ducked under their fence and approached the house. He presumed it was a child, and asked his daughter to switch on the lights.

This seemed to alarm the visitor, who immediately doubled back. The couple saw that he was about 3½ feet tall, in a green suit with padded feet, and a green helmet with a transparent face-plate. Affixed to this was an antenna, and on his back was a box, attached to his belt. The figure also had a tail.

To the amazement of the watchers, the alien ducked under the fence again, pressed the front of his belt, and took off, zooming Superman-fashion, towards some flashing lights in the distance.

UFOs Down Under

Something strange was happening in the skies above Australia and New Zealand at the end of 1978. During one ten-day period, six pilots separately reported curious objects flying alongside their planes. Radar stations recorded inexplicable bleeps on their screens. Wellington air traffic controllers watched for three hours as objects darted erratically around at remarkable speeds. Above Cook Strait, ten shapes blipped across the screen, ''radically different in behavior from normal aircraft.'' Then, at midnight on December 30, a television crew aimed their camera at a blazing light approaching a plane. And experts who analyzed their amazing pictures said: ''It may be a spaceship.''

The TV crew were from Channel O in Melbourne, Australia. Anxious to check out the spate of strange sightings, they boarded an Argosy turbo-jet used to make newspaper deliveries between Wellington, Christchurch and Blenheim, New Zealand. Captain Bill Startup, an airline pilot for 23 years, had seen gleaming oval objects over the Cook Strait during his regular run a few days earlier. Now, as he flew over the same area with the TV team, they were there again. Reporter Quentin Fogarty, 32, said: ''We saw a blazing white fireball about 50 miles ahead. It was brilliantly lit at the bottom and seemed to have orange rings round it.'' Cameraman David Crockett began shooting film as his wife Ngaire switched on the sound equipment. As the plane got closer, Crockett became convinced that the shape in his sights was not a natural one. Then he noticed smaller objects around it. They were moving in ''intelligent'' fashion. They seemed ''in control of the situation, not of this world.''

Captain Startup said: ''One object resembled a large ball of light. No aircraft would have the kind of acceleration that this thing did. It came within 18 miles of us and we decided to go in closer. It went above us and then below, and shot away at tremendous speed.'' Co-pilot Bob Guard added: ''We watched the objects for almost 20 minutes. It was almost like watching strobe lights.''

Next morning, the TV team examined the evidence. Leonard Lee, a 32-year-old documentary film producer and a senior member of the Channel O news staff, said: ''The film sent a shiver down my spine. Every time I looked at it, my whole body tingled. We realized we had obtained something absolutely phenomenal, but we decided to make no claims about it other than what our film crew had seen.''

The film was sold to countries all round the world, and screened on news bulletins. Interest in it was astonishing. For the first time, professional cameramen had captured evidence of what seemed to be a mechanical craft from somewhere other than Earth.

But there were plenty of doubters, even in Melbourne. Professor Ronald Brown, head of the city's Monash Uni-

---

Pot shots

For six years defense chiefs were baffled by the UFOs that periodically rained down on the Arizona plains. They showed up on radar at a Colorado tracking station, but when the apparent landing sites were checked, there was no sign of them.

Then, in July 1979, federal narcotics agents were told by an informer that Mexican drug smugglers were using home-made rockets to shoot marijuana across the border into America. When dates were checked, at least one drug consignment coincided with the UFO sightings.

Major Jerry Hix said at the tracking station: ''It wasn't strong enough to spark off a nuclear alert, but it did have us a bit puzzled.'' A narcotics agent said: ''It sure as hell adds a new meaning to the old saying about taking pot shots . . .''

versity chemistry department, said: "All my training as a scientist tells me the spacecraft theory is extremely unlikely. Looking at the film, I think it is quite feasible that an unusual shower of meteors could have had a similar appearance." The professor, one of the world's leading galacto-chemistry specialists, added: "It is possible that life forms exist elsewhere in the universe, but I do not believe other creatures would be able to shift a solid object such as a spacecraft at such enormous speed. An incredible amount of energy would be required to propel such a craft, and science already knows that the universe contains only a limited amount."

But TV man Lee brushed aside such skeptics. "It seems a natural reaction from certain people," he said. "They dismiss something simply because they cannot explain it." He decided to take the film to America for appraisal by UFO experts.

Navy physicist Dr. Bruce Maccabee, also a senior official with the National Investigations Committee on Aerial Phenomena agreed to study the film frame by frame. Lee arrived in America in January 1979 with his evidence in a suitcase, sealed with a secret combination, and handcuffed to his right wrist. "The very existence of this film makes it extremely important," Dr. Maccabee explained. "It has a whole lot of organizations jumping, wanting to get a look at it. So much of our work ends up in shooting down turkeys. This is one turkey that deserves the closest possible research."

He spent weeks poring over the film, examining some frames with digital computer enhancement processes. He saw a perfectly-formed glowing triangle, which he estimated to be the size of a house. Another frame showed an oval with a slight dome protruding. A third section of the film captured a circular object travelling at immense speed. Dr. Maccabee said: "The computer study unarguably shows that the images could not have come from stars or planets, or from the ground or sea surface."

The physicist also flew secretly to New Zealand to interview the eye-witnesses. "I didn't want anyone to know about the project," he explained. "It had been given a lot of publicity earlier in the year, and I wanted to do my

Mr. Jimmy Carter

Grenada's Mr. Eric Gairy   Actress Elke Sommer

Boxer Muhammad Ali

Celebrity sightings

One film star who has seen a UFO is German-born actress Elke Sommer, who in 1978 was in the garden of her Los Angeles home when a shiny orange ball, about 20 feet in diameter, appeared out of the blue. "It was glowing and floating about like a big moon," she said. "It came towards me and I fled into the house. When I reappeared, it had vanished."

Boxer Muhammad Ali was on a training session in New York's Central Park in 1972 when he encountered a UFO. He said: "I was out jogging just before sunrise when this bright light hovered over me. It just seemed to be watching me. It was like a huge electric light bulb in the sky."

Statesmen and politicians who have seen UFOs include John Gilligan, Governor of Ohio, who in 1973 reported seeing a UFO near Ann Arbor, Michigan. He described it as "a vertical shaft of light which glowed amber."

Sir Eric Gairey, Prime Minister of the Caribbean island of Grenada, tried unsuccessfully in 1978 to have the United Nations officially investigate UFOs. He said he himself had seen one—"a brilliant golden light travelling at tremendous speed."

But the most famous UFO spotter of all is Jimmy Carter who, while still Governor of Georgia, in 1973, was sitting out on a verandah with 20 other people after an official dinner at Thomastown when, in his words, they witnessed a UFO "which looked as big as the Moon and changed colour several times from red to green." He launched a $20 million study into UFOs after becoming US President.

Lord Dowding's admission

The Royal Air Force's late Air Chief Marshal, Lord Dowding, was a staunch believer in UFOs. As early as 1954, he said: "I have never seen a flying saucer, yet I believe they exist. Cumulative evidence has been assembled in such quantity that, for me at any rate, it brings complete conviction.

"There is no alternative to accepting the theory that they come from an extra-terrestrial source. For the first time in recorded history, intelligible communication may become possible between the Earth and other planets."

Although Dowding admitted never having seen a flying saucer, he would have received numerous reports of UFO sightings by the fliers under his command during World War Two.

inquiries with a minimum of fuss." He taped statements from Captain Startup and his co-pilot, from cameraman Crockett and his wife, and from reporter Fogarty, who had been admitted to hospital after being emotionally drained by the entire episode.

Dr. Maccabee also listened to tapes of conversations between Captain Startup and air traffic controllers, who had spotted inexplicable objects on their radar screens on the evening in question. "All the witnesses agreed to submit to lie detector tests if their veracity was questioned," he said.

Finally, the Navy expert concluded that the film and the interviews were a significant advance in UFO research. Stanton Friedman, a nuclear physicist and another of America's foremost aerial phenomena experts, added: "We are definitely dealing with a genuine unidentified flying object. What makes this sighting so important is not just the film, but the wealth of additional evidence. Few reported sightings have ever had so much attention focussed on them, and the quality and quantity of the research has been impressive."

The Channel O film was not the only pictorial evidence of UFOs during the spate of sightings early in 1979. A New Zealand camera team took to the air, and filmed "an illuminated ping-pong ball, rotating, pulsating and darting around" over South Island. And private detective José Duran filmed what he described as "a man from outer space" from the garden of his home near Adelaide, Australia.

UFO experts who examined Duran's cine-pictures agreed that they seemed to show a "human embryo-like" object disembarking from a flying saucer and hovering between two "spacecraft." Duran said he first saw a red and amber light, moving slowly from the north-west towards the southeast.

"I watched through binoculars for a little while, then the light seemed to approach me," he added. "I filmed it from the garden. There was a strange kind of flashing, and although it was travelling very slowly with no sound, I thought at first it might be a plane.

"To my surprise, when I developed the film, I saw something I hadn't actually noticed when I was taking it. There was a white object travelling from an angle. It stopped for a couple of seconds above what I thought was a plane. It made a jerking movement above the flashing light, then moved off in a different direction. The whole movement on film looks like a large V-sign. Moving between the spacecraft was a humanoid, flesh-coloured at one end, but the rest of its body covered in a blue shroud. Microscopic examination of the film has shown two more humanoids in and around the spacecraft."

Experts from Contact International, the British UFO research body, spent months analyzing the film, and decided that the balls of light were probably alien craft. Research officer Derek Mansell said: "The lights cannot be those of aircraft, and space agencies have confirmed that there was no debris entering the Earth's atmosphere at that time and place."

More sightings in 1979

UFO sightings in early 1979 were not confined to Australasia. From Israel came reports of a rash of red balls and flashing lights. In northern Italy, dozens of villages on the slopes of the Gran Sasso mountains were plunged into darkness after a UFO was seen hovering over a hydro-electric plant. Technicians said their equipment suddenly went haywire.

In America, TV reporter Jim Voutrot was amazed when he read about the New Zealand pictures. For he too had captured UFOs on film, at around the same time. And his shots were remarkably similar.

It happened as Voutrot cruised near Pease Air Force Base, a Strategic Air Command bomber post in New Hampshire, with Betty Hill, the woman who claimed she was abducted by aliens in 1961. "She was telling local meetings on her lecture circuit that UFOs were being sighted over the air base," Voutrot explained. "Several reporters did stories with Betty, but I'm a skeptic, and wanted to do one when I was sure there was no chance of being set up.

"So I called Betty one day and we were out looking about five minutes later. Suddenly we saw a big, round white object in the sky. I was surprised and bolted out of the car to start filming. Then, all of a sudden, it was gone. I haven't the faintest idea what it was—quite honestly, I've never seen anything like it, before or since. But I know it wasn't the Moon or Venus, it wasn't aircraft landing lights, and it wasn't a balloon."

Mrs. Hill said: "We were driving up a hill, just a hop and a skip from Pease, when Jim yelled, 'There's one.' He was out of the car before I could stop it, and was filming." When the 15-second film was magnified and examined, investigators discovered an undetected second object in the sky, with a tail of light behind it, like a comet. Further magnification disclosed yet more similar tailed lights, just

Clear for landing

The town of Arès, in the French Bordeaux region, has made UFOs an offer it hopes they will not refuse—a safe spot to land. Engineer Robert Cotton, who works at Bordeaux Airport, came up with the idea for the Ovniport. He believed UFO pilots were reluctant to land because ordinary airports get too crowded. He persuaded officials at Arès to set aside land on the town borders for a landing strip. "We have installed a number of landing lights and markings so we believe it can easily be spotted by UFO pilots," said the mayor of Arès, Christian Raymond. So far, none have arrived to entertain the tourists who regularly turn up to watch and hope.

as on the New Zealand film. And the fast, erratic movements of the larger light defied explanation.

Voutrot checked with sources at the Pease base, and found that nothing had been reported, visually or from radar watches. Tower staff told him their air space often played host to unidentified pieces of "junk." Air Force spokesmen were also unable to help. But CIA documents have revealed unexplained objects sighted over air bases in Maine, Montana and Michigan in the past.

The most incredible report of a sighting from that period came from South Africa. In January 1979 Mrs. Meagan Quezet, a former nurse, said a pink unidentified object landed near her home in Krugersdorp, west of Johannesburg—and a squad of dark-skinned little men emerged from it.

Mrs. Quezet said she saw them just after midnight, as she took her son André, 12, for a walk because he could not get to sleep. "As we walked down the road, we both saw a pink light come over the rise," she said. "Suddenly we came across this thing standing in the road about 20 yards away. In front of it were five or six small beings. These people were dark-skinned, as far as I could tell. One of the men had a beard and seemed to be the leader.

"I said hello to one of them, but I couldn't understand what he was saying. I told André to run off and bring his father, and as he did so the creatures jumped about 5 feet into the air and vanished through a door into their craft. The door slid closed and the long, steel-type legs began to stretch out. Then it disappeared into the sky with a humming noise."

Both Mrs. Quezet and her son said the craft had bright pink lights on either side of the door. The humanoids appeared to be wearing white or light pink suits and white helmets.

Many scientists and astronomers around the world poured scorn on this flurry of UFO sightings. They dismissed them as an unusual concentration of meteors, or space debris burning up on entering the Earth's atmosphere. Sir Bernard Lovell, director of Britain's Jodrell Bank radio astronomy station, said the reports were "pure science fiction." But, as we shall see, the facts about UFOs were often even stranger than fiction.

2

Encounters of the Closest Kind

Millions of people claim to have seen
flying saucers. A few believe they have
had even closer encounters. They are the
people who suddenly realize they cannot
account for a missing phase of their lives.
Many re-live the lost hours or days under
hypnosis . . . and sensational stories
emerge that really are out of this world.

Murder by forces unknown

Who or what dumped the body of Zygmunt Adamski on top of a coal pile 30 miles from his home? Why were parts of his body burned with a corrosive substance that forensic experts could not identify? And where was he for the five days after he had last been seen alive?

Those were just three of the questions West Yorkshire police were still trying to answer when Coroner James Turnbull recorded an open verdict on what he called "quite the most mysterious death I have ever investigated." Adamski's widow said: "I don't think I will ever know what happened to my husband."

Then, five months later, a West Yorkshire policeman revealed that he had seen an unidentified flying object in the town where the body was found. Under hypnosis, he told a harrowing story of being beamed on board the craft for a terrifying medical examination. And the suspicion dawned that perhaps Adamski had been put through the same ordeal—and proved not strong enough to take it.

Adamski was 56, a Pole who fled to England when the Nazis invaded his country during World War Two. He and his wife Lottie, who was confined to a wheelchair, lived in a quiet crescent in the Tingley suburb of Leeds, and it was from there that he set out on foot on June 11, 1980, to buy a bag of potatoes at a local shop. He never returned.

Five days later, Trevor Parker was loading his truck for the last delivery of the day at his father's coalyard in Todmorden. To his horror, he found a body. "It was just lying there in plain sight," he said. "I didn't know whether the man was dead or alive, so I called the police and an ambulance. I was very frightened, I didn't want to be out there myself. The body gave me a very eerie feeling.

"I have no idea how the man got in the yard, but I know one thing for absolute certain—there was no body on that coal pile when I loaded my truck earlier in the day."

Consultant pathologist Dr. Alan Edwards told police the

victim had died from a heart attack. A mysterious corrosive had burned his scalp, neck and back of the head, but his face and clothes were untouched, indicating that the substance had been applied carefully, and while the top of the body was naked. Adamski, when found, was wearing a jacket, but no shirt. There was £5 in his pocket, but his watch and wallet were missing.

The Coroner postponed the inquest three times to allow more time for inquiries, but police drew a complete blank. Mrs. Adamski told them her husband had never been to Todmorden in his life and had no connections with the town. He did not gamble, drank rarely, and was not the sort of man to make enemies. Despite frequent appeals, no witnesses came forward to say they had seen the ex-miner after June 11.

Then came news that gave the case a different and even more sinister dimension. One of the two policemen first called to the coalyard revealed that he had seen what looked like a flying saucer only hours before the body was found. He was questioned under hypnosis by UFO investigators, who confirmed his story. But West Yorkshire police refused to name him, or to let him talk to the Press.

When the inquest was at last held, Mr. Turnbull said: "As a trained lawyer, I have to rely on facts. Unfortunately, we have not been able to uncover any facts which may have contributed to this death. I tend to believe that there may be some simple explanation.

"However, I do admit that the failure of forensic scientists to identify the corrosive substance which caused Mr. Adamski's burns could lend some weight to the UFO theory. As a coroner I cannot speculate. But I must admit that if I was walking over Ilkley Moor tomorrow and a UFO came down, I would not be surprised. I might be terrified, but not surprised.

"I cannot believe that all the thousands of reports of this sort of phenomenon, covering almost every country in the world, and going back through the ages, result from human error."

Graham Birdsall, area coordinator for Contact International UK, said: "There is worldwide interest in this case—

it is the biggest UFO story for many years. The fact that the police have even considered the possibility of UFO involvement is unique.''

Walter Reid, of the British UFO Research Association, said: ''There is no obvious explanation why the body was on the pile of coal. It would seem he was literally dumped there from above.''

Adamski's widow said: ''He must have been kidnapped by someone or something, but I don't think I will ever know who or why.'' Police kept the file open, just in case . . . and on November 28 came startling new evidence that a UFO may indeed have been involved.

PC Alan Godfrey, one of the first policemen to reach the coal yard after Adamski's body was found, drove on to a Todmorden council estate at 5.15 A.M. and saw what he at first thought was a bus. Then he realized it was floating five feet above the ground, and saw that the bottom half of the shape was spinning. He saw rows of windows and a dome on top, and noted a bright blue light.

PC Godfrey, a down-to-earth father of two, tried to alert his station, but neither his car radio nor his personal walkie-talkie set would work. So he began sketching the shape. By the time he had finished, the UFO had gone. He was in two minds whether to report the incident. Then four policemen in Halifax said they too had seen the shape, and he filed his statement.

UFO researchers launched their own investigation into PC Godfrey's encounter, and discovered that 15 minutes were missing from his account. They urged him to undergo hypnosis. During the session, which was videotaped, he spoke of a shining light which blinded him. When he came round he was in a room with a table. A 6-foot figure wearing black and white was with him. He had a beard and skull cap.

Suddenly the constable was gripped by terror. John Sheard, a newspaper reporter who saw the video, described what happened next in a story in the *Sunday Mirror*. He quoted PC Godfrey as saying: ''They're horrible . . . small, 3 to 4 feet, like five-year-old lads. There are eight of them. He's touching me. He's feeling at my clothes. They have hands and heads like a lamp. They keep touching me . . . they are making noises . . . Joseph, I know him as Joseph. He has told me not to be frightened.

"They are robots, they're not humans, they're robots. They're his. They're Joseph's robots. There's a bloody dog . . . it's horrible. About the size of an alsatian . . ."

The policeman was so agitated that the hypnotist ended the session to avoid further stress. He said, "This is quite the most mysterious thing I have ever witnessed." Later, at a second session with another psychiatrist, PC Godfrey told of being examined by a machine, but when asked what it looked like, he said: "I haven't to answer that, I haven't to tell you. Each time I think about it I get a pain." After the aliens had taken off his shoes and socks to look at his toes, he found himself back in his car.

Later, PC Godfrey told Sheard, "I wish to hell all this had never happened to me. I'm just an ordinary bloke doing an ordinary job as a small-town bobby. Do you think being associated with flying saucers makes my life any easier? I've never read a science fiction book in my life."

Dr. Robert Blair, who conducted the second hypnosis session, said: "It is possible for people to lie under hypnosis or for some of them to recall some incident they have read about. But I can't see why this man should have any reason not to tell the truth—he has nothing to gain."

The death riddle and PC Godfrey's amazing evidence added up to an astonishing story. But alleged visits to alien craft are by no means uncommon. Many people say they have met and been examined by beings from other planets. Some claim they have even had sexual intercourse with them. And some have been transported thousands of miles in mysterious fashion.

Kidnapped by aliens

When shipyard workers Charles Hickson and Calvin Parker went fishing on the evening of Thursday, October 11, 1973, they expected a few quiet hours on the banks of the Pascagoula River, Mississippi. But they ended up being the catch themselves—for a UFO.

Sheriff Fred Diamond and his men could hardly believe their ears when the two men staggered into the office and told their strange tale. A curious silvery craft, about 100 feet long, had descended 30 feet from them, emitting a blue light. It had hovered just above the ground.

Then a hatch opened and three grey-looking aliens floated out. They had wrinkled skin, claw-like hands and a single slit for an eye. Parker, 19, had fainted on seeing them. But Hickson claimed he had been immobilized before being "floated aboard" the craft, and laid face up on a table. A huge electronic eye then descended and examined him from head to foot at close range. Twenty minutes later, he found himself outside the craft again.

Detectives tried to shake them out of their unlikely story, but without success. Sheriff Diamond said later: "The first thing they wanted to do was take a lie-detector test. Charlie was badly shaken. You don't see a 45-year-old man cry unless something terrible has happened. And Calvin . . . I heard that boy pray when he thought nobody could hear."

UFO investigators headed for Pascagoula as soon as news was released that the two men were having tests for radiation. J. Allen Hynek, former US Air Force consultant on UFOs and chairman of the Northwestern University's department of astronomy, flew in from New York. James Harder, professor of civil engineering at the University of California, and consultant to the Aerial Phenomena Research Organization, arrived from Los Angeles.

They heard a tape recording of the interrogation by detective Tom Huntley. The strain in the men's voices was clear. Then Huntley had left the room, but left the tape running. The two men had talked between themselves:

Parker: "I've got to get home and get to bed or see a doctor or something."

Hickson: "I've never seen nothin' like it. I can't believe it—you can't make people believe it."

Parker: "My arms just froze up and I couldn't move. Just like I stepped on a damn rattlesnake."

Hickson: "I know son, I know . . ."

Perils of washing day

A terrified Devon housewife claimed she was grabbed by aliens, and beamed onto a spaceship as she pegged washing out in her back garden in February 1978.

The woman, who asked to remain anonymous when quizzed by UFO researchers, said she first saw a blue shining shape approach her home in Ermington, near Plymouth, from the north.

"The light hovered over the garden," she said. "I was petrified. I dropped the washing. Suddenly I was completely enveloped in bubbles of light. I saw three beings who looked like men. They did not speak. They were each about five feet tall, wearing bluish metallic-like clothing.

"They grasped me by the arms and we were lifted up a beam of light into a kind of room. There were more of the men there. I was given the impression—I don't know how—that I would come to no harm.

"A little later, I found myself back on my lawn. I felt a sharp blow on the back of my neck. I was stunned but not hurt. When I looked round, the thing set off at great speed and disappeared."

The woman, identified only as Mrs. G, told her strange story to Contact UK, one of the largest British UFO investigating organisations. Bernard Delair, one of its senior members, said: "We take this report very seriously. Her story is very graphic and fits many others."

When Hickson too left the room briefly, Parker murmured: "It's hard to believe . . . Oh God, it's awful . . . I know there's a God up there . . ."

Both men underwent regression hypnosis with James Harder to verify their stories. In a trance, they confirmed

Sheriff Diamond's opinion: "They're just country boys—neither of them has enough imagination to concoct such a tale, or enough guile to carry it off." Lie-detector tests also confirmed that Hickson believed he had been taken aboard a spacecraft.

Scientist James Harder told a stunned Press conference: "The experience that they went through was indeed a real one. A very strong feeling of terror is impossible to fake under hypnosis. I've been left with the conclusion that we're dealing with an extra-terrestrial phenomenon. I can say that beyond any reasonable doubt."

Both men were found to be free of radiation, and went back to their jobs at a local shipyard. But Hickson said: "I just keep thinking, what if they'd carried us off? You'd have dragged the river and then forgotten about us . . ."

Encounter too close for comfort

John Day laughed at UFO stories . . . until the night he drove into a strange green mist and lost three hours of his life.

It happened in December 1978 as Day, a 33-year-old father of three, and his wife Sue, a 29-year-old nursery nurse, were returning to their Essex home after visiting her parents in Harold Hill.

Normally the journey took 30 minutes. They had set out at 9:20 P.M. But when they arrived, the clock on their mantelpiece showed 12:45 A.M. In the days that followed, both had recurring dreams of being on treatment tables and undergoing examinations by strange beings. The nightmares became so vivid that they were afraid to go to bed.

Finally Day contacted a UFO group, who introduced him to dentist and hypnotist Leonard Wilder. Under hypnosis, Day's subconscious revealed an amazing tale.

A white light had followed the car, landed in a field beside their route, and beamed them and the car aboard what seemed to be a spaceship. Day said he found himself in a giant room, standing beside three aliens, all 7 feet tall and

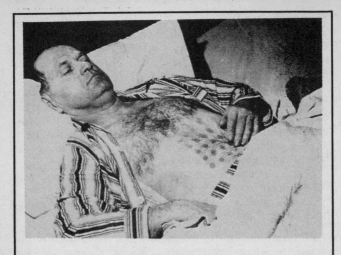

The burns on Stephen Michalak's chest and body are clearly shown. This checkerboard pattern is typical of chemical burns.

wearing silver-grey one-piece outfits which looked like body stockings. Balaclava-type hoods covered the bottom half of their faces, and they stared at him with bright pink eyes that had no eyelids.

"I found I knew what they wanted me to do," Day said. "I think they communicated with me by telepathy. I knew they wanted me to walk across the room, so I did. There was a doorway leading to another room. We all went through it.

"This was obviously an examining room, and they asked me to lie on what looked like an operating table. A metal arm swung over me, scanning my body. Then three other beings, squat and ugly like dwarfs, appeared. One started to prod me with a pen-shaped object.

"After a while, the examination seemed to be over. I asked if I could look round the ship, and they agreed. All the furniture was moulded to the wall. On one table, I saw a pile of cubes with magnets on them. They looked like some sort of game.

"At the end of the tour, the beings left me alone in another room. Suddenly an incredibly beautiful woman walked in . . . she had golden hair and was surrounded by a sort of grey mist. She walked towards me, but when I took a step towards her, she vanished. Next thing I knew I was back in the car, driving along the road.

"I had never really believed in UFOs before this happened. Now I'm convinced aliens are here and only show themselves when they want to. The ones I met kept telling me they were friendly. I enjoyed meeting them immensely."

Hypnotist Wilder said: "I have no doubt that Mr. Day is telling the truth—when I first hypnotized him, I conditioned him to tell only what really happened."

Wife Sue declined to be hypnotized—she said she did not want to relive the experience. But later, discussing her husband's statements, she recalled something of what had happened to her.

She told John Clare, a reporter for the *News Of The World* newspaper: "When I lay on the operating table they painted me with a mauve liquid. Then they washed it off. They prodded me all over with a pen-like object and didn't spare my blushes. Then I screamed.

"One of the tall beings came over and put his hand on my forehead. I went out like a light. Later they took me on a tour round the ship. They showed me a screen and said, "This is Earth." They pointed out England on it. Then we seemed to zoom in and they showed me where I lived.

"I told the beings I didn't want to go back. I asked if I could stay on the craft and they agreed. I saw John climb into the car and it started to vanish. As it disappeared, I said I had changed my mind, and wanted to go back. Then I found myself sitting in the car."

British UFO investigator Barry King said: "We have made exhaustive inquiries and are convinced that these two did indeed have a close encounter of the third kind. Some of their descriptions are similar to those given in other cases

of abduction. We can find no reason to doubt the authenticity
of their story.''

The human guinea-pigs

The curious case of Betty and Barney Hill has divided UFO
supporters and their opponents like no other. Were they
really taken aboard a spaceship for medical examinations,
or did they make it all up for publicity and profit? The
couple told a nightmarish story about what happened to them
on the night of September 19, 1961, as they drove home
through New Hampshire after a holiday in Canada. The
night was clear, and as Barney watched the road from behind
the wheel, Betty gazed out at the moonlit Connecticut River
valley, and up at the twinkling stars. Then she was startled
to note that one of the stars, bigger and brighter than the
others, was moving. It was following them.

For an hour, the craft shadowed the car. Then, at about
11 P.M., as the Hills emerged from a road in the shadow
of Cannon Mountain, they saw the bright light ahead of
them, 200 feet away over the Indian Head fields. Betty later
described it as a ''flying pancake,'' an enormous object with
two rows of portholes running around its middle. There was
no sound as it hovered.

Betty begged Barney to stop the car, and both got out to
stare at the craft. Betty stood beside their vehicle, lost in
wonder. Then she felt a sudden fear. ''Let's go,'' she said,
turning to where Barney had been. But he was not there.
He was walking towards the glowing object.

Holding binoculars to his eyes as he advanced, Barney
claimed he could clearly see creatures behind a window,
watching him as carefully as he was examining them. They
were man-shapes in shiny black jackets. And their eyes sent
a chill of horror down his spine—ice-blue, slanted and
malevolent.

He stood rooted to the spot, not hearing Betty's repeated
cries of, ''Barney, Barney, come back.'' Then the craft

A whirlwind ride

Missile engineer Daniel Fry claimed in 1950 that a smooth, oval-shaped capsule landed near him in New Mexico, and voices invited him to take a trip in it. He said he was whisked to New York and back—a round trip of 8.000 miles—in less than an hour. The voice told him that expeditions from the UFO's planet had been visiting Earth for centuries to try to help human development, but had yet to meet people who were sufficiently intelligent. Fry later claimed that the CIA suppressed his story for 12 years.

began to descend. Somehow he broke free of the spell and leapt into the car with Betty at his side. They roared away, trying to ignore a soft, beeping noise.

Both felt numb and uncomfortable, aware that something had happened, but not sure what. Barney looked at his watch and noted that it was 1 A.M. Then he passed a signpost to the town of Ashland. Two hours had slipped by since they had stopped to watch the craft. And they were 35 miles farther south than they should have been, with no way of accounting for the missing time or distance.

At first the couple decided to tell nobody of their experience. Barney said they would be laughed at as idiots. But he could not forget the incident, or the curious pains from his lower stomach and groin. After a few days, he consulted a friend who was a physicist, because he was afraid the pains might be due to some sort of radiation. The friend suggested testing their car with a compass, which would detect radiation. Barney held the instrument close to some mysterious round spots that had appeared on one of the doors. The compass needle swung wildly.

Ten days after their eerie drive home, Betty Hill began to suffer nightmares. For five consecutive nights, she dreamed of strange beings, though she could never remember the details next morning. The couple, growing increasingly worried about their physical and mental health, realized they could keep their secret no longer. In need of help, they asked to be examined by a psychiatrist.

Dr. Benjamin Simon, one of the country's foremost mind doctors, began a series of interviews. For weeks he interrogated the couple under hypnosis, constantly cross-checking their story in every detail. Eventually he was satisfied that he had unlocked the full facts of what had happened on September 19.

Barney had never turned round and run back to Betty and the car. Instead, she had joined him, and together they had walked to meet two groups of men approaching from the craft.

Betty told the doctor of telepathic assurances from the aliens. She felt trapped by their will-power, and when her terror fought against that, strong arms bundled her aboard the spaceship. They were led along a corridor to a doorway. Betty hesitated, waiting for her husband. But she hardly recognized him. He was in a deep trance.

Inside the room, an alien began a medical examination. One sleeve of her dress was rolled up, and pictures were taken of her skin. Some of the surface was gently scraped away, and samples of hair and nails were also taken. The man carefully looked at her ears, teeth and mouth, then ordered her to strip and lie flat on her back on a table.

Slowly he went over her from head to foot with a cluster of needles attached to wires. After asking her to turn over, he repeated the operation. When she was again lying on her back, he approached with a single, longer needle, and announced that he was going to insert it into her navel. Betty screamed at him not to do so, but he ignored her. The pain was terrible. But it mysteriously subsided when another man, who seemed to be the leader, rubbed his hands in front of her eyes, and told her that the pain would disappear.

Most of her fear had vanished too as she got dressed again, and she began to chat to the "doctor," who spoke English but with an accent Betty could not place. She asked for a souvenir to prove what had happened to her, but the aliens refused.

Barney could remember much less, even under deep hypnosis. But he did recall walking terrified into an examination room, and having his groin covered by some sort of cup. When it was over, he felt strangely happy and reassured, knowing they would not be harmed.

He found himself back in the car, and a minute later Betty joined him. They were both grinning, and Barney recalled thinking: "We had nothing to fear." They stayed to watch the craft rise and fly off, then carried on driving home,

---

No sign of the dog

Angler Alan Morris claims that a UFO crew kidnapped his dog. Morris, of Bethesda, Wales, told police he was fishing in a river near his home when a ball of pulsating light approached.

"It hovered for a while over where I was sitting, then landed in a nearby field," he said. "I moved closer to get a better look."

Morris said as he saw a hatch open in the side of a saucer-shaped craft. A metallic-looking ladder dropped down to the ground, and three beings climbed down it. "They were about seven feet tall, with antennae on their heads," he recalled. "They each seemed to be carrying spades and containers."

When the figures started digging, Morris's dog suddenly ran towards them. The fisherman stood up to call him back, then blacked out.

By the time he opened his eyes again, the saucer had vanished, leaving only burn marks on the spot where it had been. And there was no sign of the dog.

unaware that the two most extraordinary hours of their lives had been erased from their conscious memory.

When Dr. Simon's incredible transcripts were released, medical and military authorities began to hunt for some rational explanation. So did skeptical UFO investigators. Robert Sheaffer reported his finding 15 years later in *Official UFO* magazine.

He said that Betty's first statement had mentioned only that she had seen a UFO near the Moon, and that the couple had taken back roads home, arriving two hours later than expected. She had sketched two bright objects near the Moon, one a star, one the UFO. But on the night of September 19, Sheaffer said, there were two bright objects near the Moon—Saturn and Jupiter. If there had also been a UFO, a third would have been necessary.

Sheaffer was also dubious about Betty's nightmares. Why had they started so long after the alleged experience? And a map she had drawn, allegedly from charts of stars seen on the spacecraft, bore no relation to the known universe, despite careful analysis by astronomers.

Raymond Fowler, another UFO investigator who had painstakingly checked other sightings, also had his doubts about the story. He pointed out that later, when the Hills arranged a UFO-watch with several scientists, nothing had been seen.

Scientists argued that no one else had reported strange lights in the sky on the night of September 19. And despite Dr. Simon's high reputation, cynics claimed that hypnosis merely relaxes the mind until the patient has no control over what is said.

How does trying to debunk Dr. Simon's evidence explain the pains Barney Hill felt, or the radiation on his car?

In 1981, Mrs. Hill, then 62 and a widow since Barney's death in 1969, revealed that she had had other encounters with UFOs. She said that six weeks after the end of her hypnosis sessions, gold ear-rings lost during her September 19 visit to the spacecraft mysteriously reappeared on a pile of leaves on her kitchen table. "Obviously the humanoids found them in their ship and somehow got them back here," she said.

Mrs. Hill also said alien craft had been seen hovering over her husband's grave. "One even landed and stayed there for a few minutes," she added.

In January, 1978, she said, a UFO saved her life. She was driving across a railway line after heavy snow when a small black shape, pulsing with a ruby-coloured light, flew towards her. Frightened, she reversed the car—only seconds before an express thundered over the spot where she had been.

Mrs. Hill's last sighting came in August 1980. She claimed that she saw a UFO land beside the road. Three figures emerged from it. "I turned round to look, and my arm hit the car horn," she said. "The horn blew and the beings disappeared."

The missing days

Travis Walton was one of a group of six tree-trimmers driving home in a truck after work in Arizona's Sitgreave-Apache National Forest on November 5, 1975. Suddenly crew boss Mike Rogers stood on the brakes. A flying saucer was hovering 15 feet above nearby trees.

Despite shouted warnings from the other men, Walton leapt from the truck and ran towards the craft. A flash of blue and white light shot from it, and Walton slumped to the ground. Petrified, the men in the truck drove off, but concern for their work-mate forced them to return a few minutes later. There was no sign of him . . . or the craft.

Local police were dubious about the men's stories. They gave them lie-detector tests, and asked whether any of them had murdered Walton. The tests proved negative. Mike Rogers told detectives: "Even before I stopped the truck, Travis was out of the cab. I just sat there with the rest of the guys, looking and not believing my eyes. Suddenly I saw this bluish flash and saw Walton falling backwards.

"I hit the gas. We looked back and saw a blackness . . . I was icy and chilled . . . I could hardly see."

Police launched a massive hunt for the missing lumber-

Travis Walton recklessly ran towards the UFO that hovered above the truck in which he was going home. He was abducted and nothing was heard of him for five days. His story of his experience was tested twice by a lie detector. He failed the first test but passed on the second.

man, but found no trace of him. Then, on November 10, Walton's sister answered a call from a public phone box. It was her brother, badly shaken, and with no idea where he had been for the past five days.

Like Betty and Barney Hill, Walton was interrogated under hypnosis. This is the amazing story he told:

"I know people won't believe me, that they'll call me a freak or a crackpot. But I was in their spaceship and I met those creatures. We all saw the saucer that night. I was excited as the truck halted, and I just jumped out and ran towards the glow. I felt no fear.

"Then something hit me. It was like an electric blow to my jaw and everything went black. When I woke up I thought I was in hospital. I was on a table on my back and as I focused I saw three figures. It was weird. They weren't humans. They looked like foetuses to me, about 5-foot tall, and they wore tight-fitting, tan-brown robes. Their skin was white like a mushroom, but they had no clear features.

"I guess I panicked. I grabbed a transparent tube and

tried to smash it to use as a weapon. But it wouldn't break. I was petrified. I wanted to attack them but they just scampered away. I was alone. Then another man suddenly appeared a few feet from me. He seemed human, but he just smiled at me through a kind of helmet, like a fishbowl.

"He led me through a corridor into another big bright room. There was a high-backed chair in the middle of the room with buttons on one arm and a lever on the other.

"The man left as suddenly as he had arrived and I began to play with the buttons. I pushed the lever and the scene outside suddenly changed. I felt we were moving. I knew we were in a spaceship. Then things went black again.

"When I woke again I was shaky. I was on the highway. It was black but the trees were all lit up because just a few feet away was the flying saucer. I saw no one. I was wearing my working clothes.

"I just ran. I recognized I was in a village a few miles from my home in Heber. When I found a phone booth, I called my sister."

Walton was a Mormon, and there seemed no reason why he should be lying. But when he took a lie-detector test arranged by a US weekly newspaper, he failed it. A later test was passed.

Philip Klass, a writer for the magazine *Aviation Week*, found that suspicious when he investigated the story. He spoke to the man who conducted the first test, and was told that the story seemed "a gross deception." Klass also claimed that Walton was allowed to set the questions on the test he passed.

But why should he have lied? Klass had an answer to that, too. He accused Rogers of inventing the abduction as a means of getting out of a wood-cutting contract that could not be completed on time, and on which he faced having to pay a financial penalty.

If it was a hoax, though, how can we explain Travis Walton's state after his alleged encounter? He became a broken man with a haunted, listless look. "I wish it had never happened," he told friends. "I don't enjoy being regarded as a liar."

Four years after the Arizona incident, a French teenager

disappeared in similar mysterious circumstances. It was exactly a week before he reappeared in equally mystifying fashion.

Frank Fontaine was 19, happily married with a six-month-old baby. At 4 A.M. on Monday, November 26, 1979, he was helping two friends load a van with clothes to take to Gisors market when they all sighted a "bright and twirling light" descending. While his pals, Jean-Pierre Prevot and Saloman N'diaye, went indoors to fetch a camera, Fontaine drove the van towards the spot where the light seemed likely to land.

"When we came out, Frank's van was 200 meters away," Prevot told police later. "It was enveloped in a bright light, like a halo surrounding it. Close by were three equally bright lights. Suddenly they all converged on one spot—the van."

As the terrifying halo lifted into the sky, the two men rushed to the van. The engine was still running, the headlights were on, the door was open . . . and Fontaine had vanished.

Local police at Clergy Pontoise, Val D'Oise, at first treated the story as a joke. They questioned Prevot and N'diaye at length, individually, over the whole day, but could not shake their evidence. They checked with their families and were told that both were responsible men not given to hoaxes or practical jokes. Tests revealed that neither was drunk nor on drugs.

Baffled detectives circulated Fontaine's picture to all French forces. They checked his van for radiation, but tests proved negative. They asked air bases if any unidentified objects had been reported in the sky, and again drew a blank. For a week, nobody had any idea what had happened to the missing Fontaine.

Then, on December 3, he walked into N'diaye's flat shortly after 4 A.M. He said he had just found himself on the spot where his van had been, and assumed that it had been stolen while he had been unconscious after blacking out in the bright lights. He had no idea that a week had passed since that incident . . . he thought it was still November 26.

The two men telephoned Prevot, and together they all went to the police. If they were glad to see that Fontaine was safe, they did not show it. Instead, hard-headed detectives interrogated him all day, convinced that the three were involved in some sort of prank.

Fontaine could remember nothing of the missing week. He recalled only driving towards the light, which approached the road from the right until it landed on the van's bonnet. It was as big as a tennis ball. He felt a strong tingling in his eyes, then everything went blank. He knew nothing of four lights converging on him.

After intensive inquiries, police had to abandon the case without finding a solution. Commandant Roger Courcous, head of the Pontoise station, said: "We are swimming in fantasy."

Visitors from a devastated planet

A family from Gloucestershire claim they were abducted by aliens from the planet Janos, who offered to share their technological secrets with Earth if they were allowed to live peacefully here. John Mann, his wife Gloria, and his sister Frances all say they saw film of the planet, and were told that it had been devastated by a chain of nuclear explosions.

Their bizarre story emerged during hypnosis sessions to try to find out what really happened as the family drove home after a visit to John's mother in Reading, Berkshire, on Monday, June 19, 1978. They set out at 9:30 P.M., with the children, five-year-old Natasha and three-year-old Tanya, dozing on the back seat of the old white Vauxhall Victor. It was 10:15 when they reached Stanford-in-the-Vale, Oxfordshire, and John, who knew the road well, was confident of reaching his home in Brockworth in another hour.

But as they went up a small rise beyond the village, he noticed a brilliant white light in the sky about a mile ahead. The two women saw it too, and agreed it was too large to be a star. After another mile, with the light maintaining its distance, John stopped the car to listen for any noises. Suddenly a red light flashed to the right of the white light, which seemed to be getting larger. The Moon, which had been full, blacked out at the same moment, and John heard a sound, "a mixture of a swishing sound and the scoring noise of a train's wheels against the track."

He went on: "The Moon reappeared and I could make out a vast circular shape over 100 feet up, moving very slowly. It came directly at us, went over the car, and drifted over trees on the right into a field. As it swung away we could see a massive saucer-shaped object, its undercarriage lit by a circular rim of brilliant coloured lights."

His wife's shouts brought him out of a dream. "Quick, John, get in the car, it's going to land." He drove off. But after 100 yards, he realized they were no longer on the familiar A417. "It was pitch black, and we were tightly hemmed in by a tall, dense hedge I could not see over," he recalled. "The road was no longer straight, but wound up and down small humps and rises, with sharp bends. I had the strange feeling that if I took my hands off the wheel, the car would drive itself."

They rounded another bend, and found themselves in Faringdon. It was unusually quiet for 10:30, pub-closing time, and John could not recall passing the Faringdon sign at the entrance to the town. As they drove on towards Cirencester, Frances noticed the same ball of white light, keeping pace with them 200 yards to the right. It disappeared whenever the car came close to houses, and finally vanished for good at Cirencester.

When he arrived home 20 minutes later, John rang RAF Brize Norton, about seven miles from Faringdon, to report the UFO. As he looked at his watch, he got a shock. It was after midnight, and they should have been home an hour earlier. Frances insisted on driving on alone to her home and her husband Ronald in nearby Stroud. The Manns put the children to bed and turned in themselves, both feeling a little baffled and sick.

The following evening, John returned from his work as a building contractor, and decided to retrace their journey to look for the mystery road bounded by hedges. He couldn't find it. He went back at the weekend to examine the field where he thought the UFO had landed. There were no marks. Had it all been just a dream?

Over the next few days, John developed a heat rash on the lower part of his chest, and his wife found similar marks on her left arm and leg. They checked with Frances, and she too had been scratching irritated skin. Even more peculiar, they all had unexplained bruises just below the right knee.

A week later, Natasha woke in the night crying and confused, calling: "Where is my Mummy? I want my Mummy." It was the first of four nightmares the little girl had over the next fortnight. Her mother asked her what they were about.

"She told me she could see lots of strange people with funny eyes staring at her," Gloria said. "Someone had taken Mummy and Daddy into other rooms. When I tried to get more out of her, she got very cross, and said, 'You should know, you were there.'"

The dream convinced John Mann that something strange had happened during that missing hour on their journey home. Both he and sister Frances decided to undergo hypnosis to try to unlock their subconscious memories. Hypnotherapist Geoffrey M'Cartney agreed to the sessions . . . and the result was a story that startled the world.

John recalled that the UFO hovered in front of the car, 100 feet off the ground. Instead of driving down the darkened road, he had stopped and got out, walking into a white mist. At least eight shadowy and silent figures passed him, walking to the car and returning with the women and the children.

"Together we all walked towards a brilliant column of light," John said. "As we entered the light beam, we seemed to float upwards. I was then in a circular room with three men wearing close-fitting metallic silver suits with balaclava-type helmets. They had pale blue eyes and pale complexions.

"One of them welcomed us in English, and told me they wished to examine me. He said no harm would come to us.

I left the others and went into another room where there was a sort of dentist's chair. A woman strapped my arms to the chair arms while another pressed buttons at a desk.

"An intense beam of light shone into my face, then one of the women pulled something black down from the ceiling and I was completely dazed. When I woke up, a man came into the room and talked to the women in a language I could not understand. Then he introduced himself as Anouxia, and told me to follow him back to the first room. He spoke into a recessed wall microphone in his own language, and about 50 people entered the room.

"Anouxia told me in English that something was coming, and the ship had to move a short distance. He said we were lucky to be in the engine room while it moved. The floor tipped to the left.

"Later I asked how the ship was powered, and he said it was a process they were prepared to bargain in exchange for the chance of living peacefully on Earth. He then took me to what he called the navigation room, switched on a screen, and said he wanted to show me pictures of his home.

"I had the impression the film was being taken from an aircraft coming in to land, and I felt I was actually on board. We flew over a desolate landscape of grey boulders and rocks, and I could see some of the rocks parting and a craft emerging, about the size of a single-decker bus. It went into a tunnel. Then I saw six figures dressed like monks carrying a crate. Anouxia said the crate was a coffin—the craft had come to collect their dead. I felt terribly sad."

Frances too was given an examination. Then a man called Uxiaulia, who had a plain white disc on his silver uniform, told her he was an explorer pilot from the planet Janos, and wanted to show her film which would explain why they had left to seek somewhere else to live.

"There were three planets on the screen, which he called Sarnia, Sarton and Janos," Frances recalled. "Apparently Sarton, the one nearest their sun, came too close to Janos and started to disintegrate, showering them with meteorites. When one hit a nuclear power station, it set off a chain reaction which devastated the planet."

The next picture, according to Frances, was of a young

blonde woman and two children. Uxiaulia told her they were his wife, son and daughter, who all died in the explosions. Then he said survivors from Janos had escaped on a master base ship, and were sending out explorer ships to find a new home for their people. "From what they had seen of Earth, they would like to live here," said Frances.

Both she and John remembered being given colourless fizzy drinks before they left the ship. "It is to help you forget," they were told. "You must forget because you will be exploited. In time you will remember. We will meet again, and you will know us."

Was it all just a wild science-fiction story? Scientists and doctors checked out the family's experiences, and their hypnotherapist was convinced they believed they were telling the truth. The consistency of their stories, told separately, also lent credence to them, especially when little Natasha, who had not been hypnotized, told her story to newspaper writers—a story that matched in every detail.

Strangers from the sea

In November 1980, a concert pianist and her friend claimed that they had been whisked aboard a UFO and given a gruelling examination. Again the full story came out only after hypnosis sessions.

Luli Oswald, 55, said she and Fauze Mehlen, 25, were driving along the coast road near Rio de Janeiro, Brazil, when they saw a fleet of strange craft emerge from the ocean. "When they came out of the water, it was like a mushroom with water spilling over it," she told police. "Then we noticed a big black one ahead of us. It seemed to be about 300 feet across with a small dome on top."

Mehlen, who was driving, lost control of the car. It began weaving crazily across the road, with the doors opening and shutting by themselves. Then, suddenly, the nightmare ended. Shaken, they stopped at a restaurant for coffee . . . and discovered that it was two hours later than they thought.

"The man was panicked and she was trying to calm him

down," a restaurant spokesman said. "They told me what had happened, and I told them that others have had trouble on that curve of road. One of my friends was chased by a UFO there."

Miss Oswald went to a top hypnotist, Dr. Silvio Lago, in an attempt to fill the two-hour gap in her memory. "I can see two small UFOs above us," she said when under his influence. "I'm feeling sick, nauseated. Our car is being grabbed by the top. A light from the small ones is holding us, the light clasps the car. We're being held prisoners by this light. It's horrible . . ."

The pianist began sobbing with terror as she continued to relive the experience. "We have entered the black disc from the bottom," she said. "The car is inside the UFO, but we are outside the car. They are putting a tube in my ear. There are tubes everywhere . . . they are pulling my hair.

"They look like rats . . . oh, how horrible! They have huge, horrible rat ears and their mouths are like slits. They are touching me all over with their thin arms. There are five of them, their skin is grey and sticky . . ."

Miss Oswald said she saw Mehlen lying unconscious on a table as the aliens examined him with a strange ray of light that smelt of sulphur. The rat figures communicated without speaking, but she said one of them did talk to her. "He said they came from Antarctica," she recalled. "There is a tunnel that goes under the South Pole, that's why they come out of the water. Others are extra-terrestrials."

After two hours, the examinations were over, and the couple found themselves mysteriously back in the car and on Earth.

"You will forget everything . . ."

A 16-year-old American high school boy reported seeing a space creature in his backyard. He described the creature as being very tall, with large green eyes and no nose. The boy said he stepped from his back door and walked towards the visitor . . . and remembered no more until he awoke the next day.

The boy agreed to undergo tests at the Southwest Montana Mental Health Centre, Annaconda. The youth had forgotten what happened after he encountered the creature, but under hypnosis he revealed that three aliens had dragged him into a spacecraft. They had examined him under a bright light and then told him he would forget the entire incident.

Dr. Kent Newman, who conducted the experiment, said: "I believe that boy honestly reported what he had experienced."

A similar view is taken by Dr. Leo Sprinkle of the University of Wyoming, Laramie, whose tests revealed that most space encounters took place against the subjects' wills and that they were generally terrified and highly emotional. They often experienced physical effects and amnesia.

Dr. Sprinkle said: "I don't know whether these people experienced physical or out-of-the-body encounters, but my personal and professional bias is to accept their claims as real."

Dr. Alfin Lawson, of California State University, Long Beach, is more cautious. After placing several abduction witnesses under hypnosis, he said: "Their stories are at least partially true. But that does not mean that their experiences are necessarily 'real' physical events—any more than hallucinations are."

The price of passion

Aliens from other planets have hijacked men and women for sex during visits to Earth. That is the incredible claim of British UFO Research Association investigator Barry King.

He reported the case of a lady from Taunton, Somerset. She alledged that she was driving at night near her home when her car engine cut out. As she got out to look under the bonnet, she was seized from behind, and fainted.

She came round to find herself naked and bound to a table, a blue blanket covering her. Three men in pale blue tunics, all around 5 ft. 6 in. tall, with fair skin and round, emotionless eyes, conducted a medical examination. Then two left.

Mrs. X. claimed the man who stayed with her placed a small pin-like device on her thigh, which made her feel numb and semi-paralyzed. He then raped her, calmly and without emotion. Mrs. X. passed out again, and next found herself lying beside her car. The engine worked perfectly.

"She drove home and told her husband the whole story," Mr. King said. "She is a level-headed woman, and I am satisfied she is telling the truth. I believe such cases happen more frequently than we know. Many victims would be very unwilling to talk about it."

A Brazilian farmer was certainly reluctant to talk about his close encounter of the intimate kind—until he was forced to go to the authorities with radiation sickness.

The man had an extraordinary story to tell. He claimed a shining egg-shaped capsule landed in one of his fields on the cold starlit night of October 15, 1957. A group of humanoids in close-fitting grey overalls and grey helmets bundled him aboard the craft, stripped him, sponged him with a freezing cold liquid, then took a blood sample from his chin with a suction cup.

He lay naked and frightened on a couch after they left. Then a naked woman appeared, a woman unlike any he had seen before. Soft, blonde hair framed a triangular face with large blue, almond-shaped eyes and a pointed chin.

She had a well-formed figure, a narrow waist, broad hips and long legs. The prisoner thought her the most beautiful creature he had ever seen. She smiled down at him, then put her arms round him and began to rub her face and body against him.

"Alone with this woman, who clearly gave me to understand what she wanted, I became very excited," the man later told the authorities. "I forgot everything, seized the woman and responded to her caresses.

"It was a normal act and she behaved like any other

woman, even after repeated embraces. But she did not know how to kiss, unless her playful bites on my chin had the same meaning.

"Finally she became tired and was breathing heavily. I was still excited but now she withheld herself from me. Before she left, she turned and pointed first to her belly, then with a kind of smile at me, and finally at the sky in a southerly direction."

At first, the young farmer told only his mother about the curious experience. He thought no one else would believe the strange tale. He could hardly believe it had happened himself.

But in the days that followed, his health deteriorated quickly. Nausea and headaches kept him indoors. His eyes burned and he could not sleep. Then small red circles appeared all over his body.

Local doctors who examined him called in a specialist from Rio de Janeiro. He confirmed their tentative diagnosis—the farmer had been exposed to radiation. And the dark scars and thin, tender skin on his chin were evidence of blood-letting.

The doctor was convinced that his patient was not inventing his wild story. He told skeptical police officers: "There is a complete lack of any direct or indirect signs which might indicate mental illness."

Over the seas and far away

Some people abducted by UFOs have found themselves landed hundreds of miles from where they were picked up. Waiter Carlos Diaz was walking home from work in Bahia Blanca, Argentina, early in the morning of January 4, 1975, when he was suddenly blinded by a pulsating light and heard a whine like a radio wave. He said later that the air and even the street seemed to vibrate violently. Then he felt himself being lifted off his feet and carried into the air. When he was 10 feet up, he looked down—and passed out.

He woke in what seemed to be a bright, glowing sphere. As if in a dream, he saw three silent, green-skinned creatures standing nearby. They plucked tufts of hair from his head, and it did not hurt.

Four hours after he was whisked from the streets of Bahia Blanca, Diaz was found lying dazed beside a road in Buenos Aires, 500 miles away. Close to him was a bag containing his working clothes and a newspaper he had bought in his home town that morning. He was rushed to a nearby hospital, and doctors found him to be in good health, if a little shocked. They could not understand how hair had been tugged out of his head without damaging the roots.

Seven years earlier, Dr. Geraldo Vidal and his wife were driving near Bahia Blanca when something peculiar happened. Hours seemed to shoot by in seconds. When the spell was broken, they were still driving, but the road and scenery had changed. They stopped to check their whereabouts and eventually found they were in Mexico.

The couple could not account for being 3,000 miles from home. They had no recollection of bright lights, no feeling of being lifted into the air. And they were as mystified as Mexican motor mechanics by the strange scorch marks on the bodywork of their car.

Jose Antonia da Silva remembered more about what happened to him after he vanished from Vitoria, Brazil, on May 9, 1969. He had an astonishing story to tell those who found him wandering, dishevelled and trance-like, in Bebedouro, 500 miles away, four days later.

He said creatures about 4 feet tall had plucked him from the ground and carried him off to another planet. Incredulous Brazilians had to admit that something odd had happened to him. He was clearly frightened, constantly darting his eyes skywards, and terrified of bright lights.

All three of these mystery journeys happened during the UFO age after World War Two, when most people had read of eerie experiences in their newspapers. But what can have been the thoughts of the soldier who was found stumbling in bewilderment around Mexico City's main square in 1593—kitted out with the uniform and weapons of a regiment stationed more than 9,000 miles away?

Questioned by the Inquisition, he said he had no idea how he got to Mexico, no sensation of travelling, and only a dim memory of a few blank seconds. His last recollection was of standing outside the Presidential Palace of Manila in the Philippines on sentry duty, and being told that the governor had just been assassinated. Three months later a ship from the Far East arrived in Mexico with the news that the governor had been murdered on October 25—the very day the soldier had been found in the square.

The Inquisition was also called in when a businessman mysteriously arrived in Portugal in 1655, and claimed that just seconds earlier, he had been outside his office in Goa, on the east coast of India. His last memory was of finding himself suddenly whisked into the air. The priests decided he must have occult powers—and burned him at the stake.

In the early 17th century, almost 300 years before the invention of the airplane, an 18-year-old nun told her superiors at a small convent in Agreda, Spain, that she had been flown to Central America. While there, said Sister Mary, she had converted an Indian tribe called the Jumano to Christianity. During one flight she had seen the Earth, a spinning sphere, below her.

Such words seemed like heresy. Her fellow nuns burned the diary in which she wrote details of the journeys, and officers of the Holy Office gently urged her to retract her claims. She refused.

In 1622, indignant letters were received by Pope Urban VIII and King Philip IV of Spain. They came from Father Alonzo de Benavides, a missionary sent to New Mexico. He demanded to know why he had been sent to do a job that already seemed done. The Indians had rosaries and crosses and knew how to celebrate Mass. They said that a lady in blue had taught them when she brought the religious articles. Neither the Pope nor the King knew what the missionary was talking about.

In 1630, Father de Benavides returned to Europe and heard the story of Sister Mary's flights. He travelled to Agreda and questioned her at length. Incredibly, she gave him accurate accounts of villages, people and customs he had seen in New Mexico. She told him of events and local lore that few outsiders could know. And when the missionary produced a chalice used by the Indians, Sister Mary's superiors identified it as one missing from the convent.

The nun had clearly not invented the story, but how had it happened? If we are not to dismiss the documented incident as a Catholic propaganda exercise, the only feasible explanation is that she travelled by UFO, possibly without realizing it.

Attacked by aliens

Forestry worker Bob Taylor was shocked and bleeding as he told police of his strange encounter in a Scottish wood. He said two bizarre-looking creatures had tried to drag him into their craft, but he had fought to stop them. He had no way of knowing whether he succeeded.

Taylor, the 50-year-old father of seven grown-up children, worked for the Development Corporation at Livingston, West Lothian. Early on Friday morning, November 9, 1979, he and his placid red setter were alone on Dechmont Hill when he became aware of a strong and curious smell of chemicals. As he approached a clearing to investigate, the dog started barking furiously. Taylor emerged from the trees to see an object that looked like a spacecraft.

Suddenly two aliens appeared from it. They were, he said, like landmines or wheels with arms. They approached Taylor slowly, then grabbed at his trousers, ripping them at the seams, and leaving scratch marks on his legs. The frightened forester tried to fight them off, then passed out. When he woke, both they and the craft had vanished, but he had dim memories of being pulled unconscious towards it. Eventually, Taylor struggled the few hundred yards to his van; but the wheels stuck fast in mud as he reversed, and he abandoned the vehicle to stagger the mile and a half to his home.

Police sealed off the hill while careful checks of the area were made. They found Taylor's van with the engine still running—in his panic he had forgotten to switch off the ignition. In the clearing, they found several deep triangular marks in the ground, and two parallel caterpillar tracks. Nearby were two small ruts which could have been made by the heels of someone being dragged.

Taylor's boss Malcolm Drummond also checked the secluded clearing, and was puzzled by the absence of any marks leading to the triangular indentations. He said: "Bob Taylor is not a man to make something up. If he says he was attacked by some creatures, then there must have been something there. Bob was shocked and upset by the incident." West Lothian police said: "We're taking this seriously. The marks in the ground look as if they were made by the legs of some machine."

Later the same day, a 72-year-old Glasgow woman reported seeing a pale white ball in the sky. Mrs. Mary Hunter, of Easterhouse, said: "I called a neighbour and we watched it for some time. I am sure I saw it split up in half and come together again, then suddenly it just vanished." She added: "I don't drink so I wasn't seeing things."

3

Encounters of the Historical Kind

We tend to think of UFOs as a modern phenomenon. In fact, scientists and astronomers have been logging inexplicable objects in the skies for centuries. Until man himself learned to fly, he had no way of knowing what those objects might be. Today, our own knowledge of space travel opens the way to new interpretations of old sightings— and to new answers for some of the most baffling mysteries in history.

Puzzles of the past

Though reports of UFOs have increased dramatically in the last 40 years, they are by no means unique to the 20th century. Researchers have documented more than 300 sightings before 1900. Monks at St. Albans in Hertfordshire saw "a kind of ship, large, elegantly shaped and well-equipped, and of a marvellous colour" on the night of January 1, 1254. And in 1290, the abbot and monks of Byland Abbey, Yorkshire, noted "a large round silver disc" flying over them.

Author W. Raymond Drake, of Sunderland, Tyne and Wear, who has written many books on UFOs, says: "The belief in beings from the skies who surveyed our Earth persisted in human consciousness throughout the Middle Ages." The most spectacular display from that time was probably the one recorded at Basle, Switzerland, on August 7, 1566. Giant glowing discs covered the sky, to the consternation and amazement of the locals.

In March 1716, Sir Edmund Halley, the British astronomer who gave his name to the world's most famous comet, reported seeing a brightly lit object over London for two hours.

On December 11, 1741, Lord Beauchamp claimed he watched a small oval ball of fire falling over London. About 750 yards up, it suddenly leveled off and zoomed eastwards, its long fiery tail trailing smoke as it rapidly disappeared.

And on March 19, 1748, Sir Hans Sloane, later president of the Royal Society, observed a dazzling blue-white light with a reddish-yellow tail dropping through the evening sky. It was, he said, "moving more slowly than a falling star in a direct line."

A stream of saucer-shaped objects were seen flying over the French town of Embrun on September 7, 1820. Witnesses reported that they too changed direction, performing a perfect 90 degree turn without breaking their strict for-

85

Spectacular black globes were seen over Basle, Switzerland on August 7, 1566.

mation. And in 1882, astronomer William Maunday saw a huge disc moving quickly as he studied the north-east horizon from London's Greenwich Royal Observatory. It passed the Moon, he said, then changed into a cigar shape.

In America, too, strange things happened in the sky during the 19th century. In 1878, Texas rancher John Martin was out hunting south of Denison on January 22 when he saw an object coming down from the sun, "about the size of a large saucer."

Nine years later, in April 1897, more than 10,000 people were said to have seen an airship over Kansas City, Missouri. Charles Fort, who had also reported a "large, luminous craft" over Niagara Falls back in 1833, wrote of the Kansas sighting: "Object appeared very swiftly then appeared to stop and hover over the city for ten minutes at a time. Then, after flashing green-blue and white lights, it shot upwards into space." The same craft was reported over Iowa, Michigan, Nebraska, Wisconsin and Illinois. The *Chicago Record* newspaper reported that it actually landed in fields near Carlinville, Illinois, but took off when curious townsfolk approached.

Alexander Hamilton, a member of the House of Representatives, had an even more incredible story to tell. He made a sworn statement to the effect that on April 21, 1897, he was awakened by a strange noise outside his home in Le Roy, Kansas, and watched a 300-foot cigar-shaped craft, with a carriage underneath, land near his farm. "The carriage," he said, "was made of glass or some other transparent substance alternating with a narrow strip of material. It was brilliantly lighted and everything within was clearly visible. It was occupied by six of the strangest beings I ever saw. They were jabbering together, but I could not understand a word they said." Hamilton said he and two of his men tried to move even closer to the craft, but the beings turned on some strange power, and the UFO soared up into the sky.

Both Britain and New Zealand seemed besieged by UFOs in 1909. People in more than 40 towns across Britain reported strange shapes and lights in the sky, most of them during the third week in May. At Caerphilly in Wales, a man said he met two curious figures in fur coats as he walked near his home at 11 P.M. on May 18. "They spoke in excited voices when they saw me, then rushed back to a large cylindrical object which lifted off the ground and disappeared."

The New Zealand sightings were almost all of cigar-shaped objects. Hundreds of people reported them over both the North and South Islands, by day and at night, during the six weeks from the end of July to the start of September. In February 1913 it was Canada's turn, with groups of UFOs appearing over Ontario on six separate days.

In those days, with airplanes still in their infancy, space and space travel were mere dreams, fantasies to be indulged in the pages of novels by H. G. Wells. It would take two world wars to produce the hotbed of technological invention that began to make exploration of the universe a possibility. During the 1960s and 1970s, science learned about space at first hand. And what was learned cast new light on some puzzles of the past.

The Siberian space catastrophe

It was the greatest space disaster of all time. A stricken interstellar craft changed course towards the nearest planet, its nuclear engines overheating uncontrollably. The crew were racing against time, and they lost. Just a mile from the surface, there was a blinding flash, and both they and their ship were blasted to oblivion. And it happened on Earth . . . on June 30, 1908.

That is the latest startling theory from scientists trying to explain one of the most baffling mysteries of the 20th century, the Great Siberian Fireball. For years, investigating teams returned from the desolate and devastated explosion site around the Tunguska River, unable to attribute the amazing damage they found to anything but a gigantic meteorite plunging from the heavens. Then human achievements in the arms and space races threw new light on the affair.

It was just after dawn when the fireball was first spotted. Caravans winding their way across China's Gobi Desert stopped to watch it scorch across the skies. Soon people in southern Russia picked it up, a cylindrical tube shape, glowing bluish-white, leaving a multicolored vapour trail. It was getting lower all the time. Then at 7:17 A.M. came the explosion. To the peasants of the sparsely-populated area of swamps and forests, it seemed like the end of the world.

"There appeared a great flash of light," said farmer Sergei Semenov, who was sitting on the porch of his home at Vanarva, 40 miles south of the centre of the blast. "There was so much heat that I got up, unable to remain where I was. My shirt was almost burned off my back. A huge ball of fire covered an enormous part of the sky. Afterwards it became very dark." At a nearby trading post, customers shielded their faces against the intense heat. Seconds later they were flung into the air as shock waves of enormous force reached the village. Farmer Semenov was also bowled over, and knocked unconscious. Ceilings cracked and crumbled, windows rattled and shattered. Soil was gouged out and flew through the air.

Closer to the Tunguska, the devastation was even worse. Tungus guide Ilya Potapovich had relatives who owned a herd of 1,500 reindeer. "The fire came by and destroyed the forest, the reindeer and the storehouses," he told investigators later. "Afterwards, when the Tungus went in search of the herd, they found only charred reindeer carcasses. Nothing remained of the storehouses. Clothes, household goods, harnesses . . . all had burned up and melted."

The pillar of fire that followed the explosion was seen from the town of Kirensk, 250 miles away. So were the thick black clouds that rose 12 miles above the Tunguska as dirt and debris were sucked up by the blast. The accompanying thunderclaps were heard 50 miles away. A seismographic centre at Irkutsk, 550 miles south of the Tunguska, registered tremors of earthquake proportions. Hurricane-force gusts shook windows 375 miles from the explosion. Five hours later, British meteorological stations monitored violent air waves across the North Sea. When scientists all over the world later compared notes, they discovered that shock waves from the Siberian blast had twice circled the globe. And when exploration teams arrived at the spot where it had happened, they understood why.

Virtually all the trees in an area 40 miles wide had been blown over and scorched. Giant stands of larch had been uprooted and snapped as if they were twigs. The earth, too, looked unreal. Leonid Kulik, who led the early investigations for the Soviet Academy of Sciences, reported: "The peat marshes of the region are deformed and the whole place bears evidence of an immense catastrophe. Miles of swamp have been blasted . . . the solid ground heaved outwards from the spot in giant waves, like waves in water." Kulik's researches revealed that the explosion had been seen or heard by people in an area four times the size of Britain. He revised his initial theory that the blast was caused by a single meteorite, concluding that an entire shower of meteorites was responsible.

Yet that hypothesis posed problems. Whenever meteorites

Scenes like this at Hiroshima, Japan after an atomic bomb was dropped look similar to the devastation at Tunguska, Siberia. The clue led to the atomic bomb explanation of the mystery surrounding this site.

had hit the Earth before, they had left craters. In Arizona, a hole 570 feet deep and nearly three-quarters-of-a-mile wide had been gouged by the largest one thus far known. There were other inconsistencies, too. Though trees for miles around had been blown over, some at what appeared to be the centre of the explosion were still standing, gaunt and eerie after losing their foliage and branches. In addition, some Tungus had reported finding unusual pieces of shiny metal, ''brighter than the blade of a knife and resembling the colour of a silver coin.'' Others claimed that, since the blast, their reindeer had contracted a strange new disease which produced scabs on their skins.

For years scientists argued about the fireball. Was it a gaseous comet, which would not leave a crater on impact? Was it a meteorite that had exploded in mid-air? Then, in August 1945, America exploded an atomic bomb 1,800 feet above the Japanese city of Hiroshima. And when Soviet scientist Aleksander Kazantsev saw the blitzed area, he realized he had seen scenes of identical devastation—in Siberia. At Hiroshima, trees directly under the blast still stood, while those at an angle to it were flattened, along with buildings. The mushroom cloud, the blinding flash, the shock waves, the black rain of debris—all had been noted in 1908, nearly 40 years before the nuclear age. Kazantsev was convinced that he had the answer to the Tunguska riddle. But it was far from being proved scientifically. So he alerted his colleagues to the possibilities in a novel way. He wrote a science fiction story in a magazine that mingled fact and fiction, surmising that a nuclear-powered spaceship from Mars had exploded over Siberia.

Other scientists took up the nuclear theory, though keeping an open mind about the space suggestion. They compared the Tunguska evidence with what happened when both Russia and the United States held H-bomb tests. And in 1966, Soviet investigators V. K. Zhuravlev, D. V. Demin and L. N. Demina issued a definitive paper which declared that the Siberian fireball had been, without doubt, a nuclear explosion. Further studies, both in Russia and America, revealed that the energy yield of the blast was 30 megatons—1,500 times greater than at Hiroshima.

Soviet experts examined and dismissed suggestions that the blast was caused by anti-matter or a black hole from space. In both cases, they argued, a crater would have been caused on impact. Professor Felix Zigel, an aerodynamics teacher at Moscow's Institute of Aviation, and geophysicist A. V. Zolotov both re-examined the evidence and the site, and discovered that the area of destruction was not oval in shape, as had been thought, but roughly triangular. To Zolotov it seemed that the explosive material had been in "a container" when it detonated, a shell of non-explosive material.

Professor Zigel went through eye-witness statements about the cylindrical shape, the trail of fire behind it, and the trajectory of its flight, and came to the conclusion that the object had "carried out a manoeuver" in the sky, changing direction through an arc of 375 miles, before it blew up. Soil samples from the blast site revealed tiny spherical globules of silicate and magnetite, a magnetized iron.

Dr. Kazantsev, whose science fiction story had prompted the new direction in Soviet investigations, commented: "We have to admit that the thing long known as the Tunguska Meteorite was in reality some very large artificial construction, weighing in excess of 50,000 tons. We believe it was being directed towards a landing when it exploded." The Russians claim that no UFOs were sighted for decades after the crash. When they were again reported, the craft were smaller and seemingly more manoeuvrable.

The greatest space disaster of all time? If there was a crew on the UFO, they were not the only victims of the blast. Soviet doctors believe thousands of Siberian peasants died as a result. Residents of the scattered villages around the Tunguska river were renowned for their good health and long life. Many survived long past their 100th birthdays. But after 1908, local medical men reported a big increase in "premature" deaths from "strange maladies." By the time teams investigating the nuclear explosion theory exhumed some of the long-dead bodies, science had found a name for such maladies. It was radiation sickness.

The undertaker's secret

For nearly 100 years, the secret of what undertaker William Robert Loosley saw in an English wood remained locked away in his desk drawer. But when his great, great granddaughter, clearing out her attic, discovered his report, experts were forced to the startling conclusion that a flying saucer may have visited Buckinghamshire on an autumn night in 1871.

Loosely was a highly respected member of the community of High Wycombe, now a thriving town, but in those days a small village. The undertaker woke, hot and uncomfortable, at 3:15 on the morning of October 4, and decided to take a walk in his garden to cool off. What happened next was detailed in the manuscript he locked away.

A light like a star moved across the sky, "brighter than the full moon." Then came a clap of thunder—"odd because the sky was clear." The object flew lower, stopped, then carried on descending, moving from side to side. It seemed to touch down in nearby woods.

Next morning, Loosely walked to the landing site, and after a long search, struck something metallic as he poked his walking stick into a pile of leaves. Scrabbling with his hands, he uncovered a strange metal container, 18 inches high and covered with curious knobs.

"Almost at once the thing moved a trifle," Loosely noted. "With the sound of a well-oiled lock it opened what looked like an eye, covered with a glass lens and about an inch across. Seconds later another eye opened and sent out a beam of dazzling purple light."

Then a third eye appeared, and shot out a thin rod, a little thicker than a pencil. Loosely decided to leave, but as he moved away, the machine started to follow, leaving a trail of three small ruts. The undertaker came to a clearing, and noticed that the whole surface was criss-crossed with similar ruts.

The metal box stopped briefly, and a claw shot out into the undergrowth. The purple light shone on the corpse of what seemed to be a dead rat. Then the rod sprayed liquid on the body and the rat was pushed inside a panel that opened on the side of the machine.

Loosely dropped his walking stick in his hurry to get away, and the object picked that up, too. Then it followed him into another clearing, and started herding him, "like an errant sheep," towards another, bigger metal box.

The undertaker was now close to panic. He looked up and saw a strange moon-like globe in the sky, which seemed to be signalling with lights. But before he could work out the sequence, it vanished. He fled back to his home.

As he lay in bed that night, unable to sleep, Loosely saw, through the window, a light falling into the clearing he had visited during the day. Then it rose again, and disappeared into the clouds. Baffled as to the meaning of all this, the bemused man jotted his experience down on paper, and locked the manuscript in his desk.

After it was discovered, almost a century later, science fiction expert David Langford studied the document, and later wrote a book about it. He said: "The manuscript has withstood every test of authenticity. It is clearly not a fabrication, because the man's death in 1893 absolutely rules out the possibility that he could describe the scientific concepts apparent in his tale."

Spring-Heeled Jack—
man or space monster?

Was Spring-Heeled Jack, the mysterious monster who terrorized Victorian England, really a misunderstood alien left behind by a UFO? The idea is now being taken seriously by some of those still seeking answers to one of the world's most bewildering riddles.

Spring-Heeled Jack was the nickname given to an awesome giant spotted at places from London to Liverpool during a 68-year reign of terror. Early reports of a frightening figure bounding across Barnes Common in London were dismissed as hysterical nonsense. Then, in February 1837, 25-year- old Jane Alsop answered a loud knocking on the door of her home in Bearhind Lane, Bow. She found a shadowy figure on the step, so tall that she had to raise her candle to see the face. With a bellow of agony, the visitor crashed headlong into her, loping away when her screams brought her father and sisters racing to help.

On the tombstone, with upraised arms and rage in every feature,
towered the terrific form of Spring-Heeled Jack. Freezer and Links
stood transfixed: their ghastly burden slipped slowly to the grass, but
they remained gaping, terror-struck. Vengeance had fallen!

Miss Alsop later told the police: "His face was hideous. His eyes were like balls of fire, and he vomited blue and white flames. His hands were like claws, but icy cold." She said he was wearing what looked like an oilskin garment under a black cloak, and had a fishbowl over his head.

The description tallied with similar reports from women who claimed they had been attacked on Blackheath, Barnes Common and beside Clapham churchyard. Then there was another frightening account. Lucy Scales and her sister were leaving their brother's home when they were confronted by a strange creature in Green Dragon Alley, Limehouse.

Lucy said later that a cloaked figure had sprung from the darkness, spitting flames which temporarily blinded her. Her screams summoned her brother, who found the girls sprawled half senseless on the cobblestones, then looked up to see a giant towering over him. Incredibly, the figure bounded out of sight over a 14-foot brick wall.

In January 1838, the Lord Mayor of London, Sir John Cowan, gave the monster official recognition. During a meeting at the Mansion House, he read out a letter from a panic-stricken Peckham resident who described a terrifying creature performing phenomenal feats of jumping. Immediately a flood of similar stories poured into the police from people who had stayed silent for fear of ridicule. The newspapers labelled Jack Public Enemy Number One. As sightings spread from London to the Home Counties, vigilante squads were organized and rewards offered to anyone capturing the beast. Even the Duke of Wellington, then nearly 70, went out on horseback in an attempt to hunt it down.

In February 1855, people in five South Devon towns woke to find that there had been a heavy snowfall—and that mysterious footprints had appeared in it, running for miles, over fields, along the top of walls, on rooftops and across enclosed courtyards. Some said it was the Devil. Some attributed them to a ghostly, unknown animal. Some blamed them on Spring-Heeled Jack.

In the summer of 1877, a figure which fitted his description appeared outside an army post at Aldershot. Two sentries, both crack shots, fired at almost point-blank range when he refused to halt. But he just bounded away . . .

leaving no blood on the ground where he had been hit. According to the London *Morning Post*, the intruder was "no ordinary mortal—if in fact he is mortal at all."

Four months later, residents of Newport opened fire when they cornered Jack on rooftops. Again he escaped unhurt. In Lincoln he bounded out of range when vigilantes chased him. Finally, he astounded hundreds of watchers with a display of prodigious athleticism in the Everton district of Liverpool on September 10, 1904, leaping from building to building, sometimes covering 30 feet at one jump. Then, after 15 minutes, he vaulted effortlessly over a row of terraced houses . . . and was never seen again.

For years, experts argued about Jack. Was he, as some claimed, a rich eccentric playing diabolical games? Was he an unknown animal? A phantom? Then, in July 1969, Neil Armstrong took man's first step on the Moon, watched by millions on television. A few of them saw the tremendous bounding steps of the astronaut, and remembered the story of Jack. He leapt like that. According to Jane Alsop, he had worn similar clothes—a jumpsuit and helmet. Maybe, they said, he was no ordinary mortal. Maybe he was an alien from another planet, and unaffected by Earth's gravity. And maybe he could have taught humans a lot—if only they had not greeted him with panic.

Village that disappeared

Police are still trying to discover why an entire village of 1,200 people and even the dead from their graves vanished without trace into the dark of a northern winter. The mystery began in 1930, when trapper Armand Laurent and his two sons saw a strange gleam crossing Canada's northern sky. Laurent said the huge light changed shape from moment to moment so that it was now cylindrical, now like an enormous bullet.

A few days later a couple of Mounties stopped at Laurent's cabin to seek shelter on their way to Lake Anjikuni— where, one of them explained, there was "a kind of problem.'' The Mountie asked a puzzled Laurent if the light he'd sighted had been heading towards the lake. Laurent said it had.

The Mountie nodded without further comment, and in the years that followed the Laurents were not questioned again. It was an understandable oversight. The Royal Canadian Mounted Police were already busy at that time with the strangest case in their history . . .

Snowshoeing into the village of the Lake Anjikuni people, another trapper named Joe Labelle had been oppressed by an odd sense of dread. Normally it was a noisy settlement of 1,200 people and today he'd expected to hear the sled dogs baying their usual welcome.

But the snowbound shanties were locked in silence, and no smoke drifted from a single chimney.

Passing the banks of Lake Anjikuni, he found boats and kayaks still tied up at the shore. Yet when he went from one door to another, there was only the unearthly quiet. And still leaning in the doorways were the men's cherished rifles. No Eskimo traveller would ever leave his rifle at home.

Inside the huts, pots of stewed caribou had grown mouldy over long-dead fires. A half-mended parka lay on a bunk with two bone needles beside it.

But Labelle found no bodies living or dead, and no signs of violence.

At some point in a normal day—close to mealtime, it appeared—there had been a sudden interruption in the day's work, so that life and time seemed to have stopped dead.

Joe Labelle went to the telegraph office and his report chattered into the headquarters of the Royal Canadian Mounted Police. Every available officer was dispatched to the Anjikuni area. After a few hours search, the Mounties located the missing sled dogs. They were tethered to trees near the village, their bodies under a massive snowdrift. They had died of cold and hunger.

And in what had been the Anjikuni burial ground, there was another chilling discovery. It was now a place of yawning open graves from which, in sub-zero temperatures, even the bodies of the dead had been removed.

There were no trails out of the village, and no possible means of transportation by which the people could have fled. Unable to believe that 1,200 people could vanish off the face of the earth, the RCMP widened its search. Eventually it would cover the whole of Canada and would continue for years. But more than half a century later, the case remains unsolved.

Could UFOs also be responsible for other vanishing acts over the years? In 1924 two experienced RAF pilots called Stewart and Day crashlanded in the Iraqi desert during a routine short flight. When they failed to arrive, rescue parties were sent out. They soon found the plane, and footsteps leading away from it showed that the two men had set off on foot in the direction of their destination. But after a short distance the footsteps stopped. There were no signs of a skirmish, no other footprints in the sand, no other marks at all. The men's track just stopped suddenly, one foot in front of the other, indicating that they had been walking normally when something happened. The two were never seen again.

In 1900 three tough fishermen set out from Lewis in the Outer Hebrides to relieve three lighthouse keepers at the Flannan Isles beacon. They found nothing wrong at the lighthouse. There were no hints of damage or accident, no disorder, no signs of panic, no missing boats, no loss of fuel, no messages . . . and no men. The three keepers had simply vanished off the face of the Earth.

In 1909, Oliver Thomas, an 11-year-old boy, walked out of a Christmas Eve party at his home in Rhayader—and disappeared for ever. Merrymakers dashed outside when they heard a sudden cry that seemed to come from the sky above the house, but they saw nothing.

Life on other planets

Many scientists believe that human life itself came from space—developing from viruses and bacteria brought to Earth by giant comets. Sir Fred Hoyle, for 20 years professor of astronomy at Cambridge, was scoffed at when he first put forward the theory in 1940. But now scientists all over the world believe he was right.

Hoyle was one of the first to identify giant dust clouds that float silently through space, swarming with the ingredients of life. He claimed that a comet plunged through one of these clouds 4,000 million years ago, picking up viruses and bacteria that became locked in globules of frozen water in its tail.

When the comet—our first UFO—crashed into Earth's atmosphere, friction melted the globules, and the life-forming cells were showered into the mists of the cooling planet to produce plants, animals and humans.

Dr. Chandra Wickramasinghe, of University College, Cardiff, believes that millions of comets, "dirty snowballs" of frozen gases and dust, bombarded Earth, carrying randomly constructed genetic molecules that took root here.

He pointed out to an international conference in Maryland that the Greek philosopher Anaxagoras had similar ideas in 500 B.C., arguing that the seeds of plants and animals swarmed in the universe, ready to sprout wherever they found a proper environment.

New scientific techniques have proved that the dust clouds of space contain such chemicals as methane, formic acid, formaldehyde and other substances crucial to forming simple life cells. One cloud showed traces of cellulose—the vital glue of molecular chains.

Could comets have created life on other planets, and in other forms? Dr. Sherwood Chang, of the Ames Research Centre in Mountain View, California, says that the millions of impact craters on Mars and Venus were formed mainly by comets. And in the words of Dr. Wolfram Thiemann, of the University of Bremen, West Germany: "Chemical evolution is definitely growing on other planets and in interstellar material. There is more and more evidence that there are other planets like Earth in outer space."

Sir Bernard Lovell, one of the world's leading radio astronomers, believes there are about 100 million stars in our galaxy, the Milky Way, that have the right chemistry and temperature to support organic evolution; and there are bil-

The planet Venus photographed from Mariner 10.

lions more galaxies in the observable universe. The odds against Earth being the only planet with life are therefore . . . astronomical.

Space collisions and explosions

Other planets have played a crucial part in the development of life on Earth—and are even responsible for the shape of Earth as we know it. That was the controversial theory put forward in 1950 by Immanuel Velikovsky, a Russian-born doctor and psychoanalyst who settled in America, in his book entitled *Worlds in Collision.*

Velikovsky claimed that cataclysmic disasters recorded in the Bible and echoed in the ancient writings of the Mayas, Chinese, Mexicans and Egyptians were all due to convulsions in the universe, which sent Venus and then Mars into orbits too close to Earth.

Venus, according to Velikovsky, was part of Jupiter until an explosion sent it crashing into space more than 4,000 years ago. It hurtled towards the sun, blazing brightly, and trailing a slipstream of dust and gases. Earth moved into the outer edges of this slipstream in the middle of the 15th century BC, and a fine red dust coloured our rain. ''All the water that was in the Nile turned to blood," stated the Biblical Book of Exodus. Then came showers of meteorites, and according to the Mexican Annals of Cuauhtitlan, the sky rained "not water but fire and red-hot stones."

When gases coalesced to form petroleum, "people were drowned in a sticky substance raining from the sky," in the words of the Mayas' sacred book, Popol-Vuh. Elsewhere, the petroleum was ignited by oxygen in the Earth's atmosphere, and a terrible deluge of fire was recorded from Siberia to South America.

Finally, said Velikovsky, Earth was subjected to the full gravitational pull of the new planet and was tugged off its axis. Hurricanes and floods destroyed islands, levelled cities and altered the face of continents. "Heaven and earth changed places," wrote the Cashinaua of western Brazil. The Persians watched in awe as three days of light were followed by three days of darkness.

It was then, Velikovsky argued, that Moses led the Israelites across the Sea of Passage. Freak gravitational and electromagnetic forces, as well as the convulsions of the Earth's crust, piled up the waters on either side of the seabed. As the Egyptians pursued their former slaves, a powerful electric bolt passed between Earth and Venus, and the waters flooded back into place, drowning them.

The few survivors of the worldwide catastrophes faced starvation. But suddenly food fell from the skies—manna from heaven to the Israelites, ambrosia to the Greeks, honey-like madhu to the Hindus. Velikovsky believed it was created either by bacterial action or by electrical discharges in the Earth's atmosphere working on hydrocarbons in the trail of Venus.

Just as Earth was getting accustomed to its new seasonal timings, Venus swung past again, in about 1400 BC, with equally disastrous effects. Then it settled into an orbit that left our ancestors in peace. But in the 8th century BC, it passed too close to Mars, dislodging the smaller planet, and pushing it into an orbit which clashed with that of Earth. Again there were geophysical upheavals, recorded in the Bible by the prophets Isaiah, Hosea, Joel and Amos, and in the *Iliad* by Homer. Once more the calendar had to be revised, because a year of twelve 30-day months was no longer accurate.

Velikovsky said that Mars returned every 15 years until 687 BC, the last time it caused great disturbances, when, according to the Chinese Bamboo Books, "Stars fell like rain and the Earth shook." In some parts of the world, the rising sun dipped back below the horizon as Earth again tilted on its axis. Then both Venus and Mars settled into orbits that no longer influenced us.

The controversial theory explained many aspects of ancient myth, legend and history, not least why Mars replaced Venus as predominant god among the Greeks and Romans. But it outraged scientists in 1950. One curator of a planetarium who backed Velikovsky was sacked.

Velikovsky had flown in the face not only of accepted scientific principles but of Darwin's theory of an ordered evolution. Yet in the next 30 years, as space travel revealed many more facts about Venus and Mars, his theories were proved right time and time again. He was ridiculed for saying that Venus had a comet-like tail, that it was much hotter than Earth, and that its atmosphere was far heavier than that of Earth. American and Russian probes proved the truth of his claims. He was derided for saying that Mars had a surface of craters, and that its atmosphere contained the rare gases argon and neon. Again, space explorations found he was correct.

Neither Venus nor Mars were exactly unidentified flying objects, but the powers they unleashed terrified and puzzled our ancestors. And even today there are flying objects we can identify, but which are every bit as baffling as UFOs.

The day it rained animals

By the known laws of nature, frogs, fish, mice and periwinkles do not fly. Yet all have fallen from the skies for no apparent reason, and without explanation.

At Sutton Park, Birmingham, in June 1954, shoppers in a crowded street were astonished by a deluge of tiny, pale frogs. They bounced off umbrellas and hats, fell into shopping baskets, and hopped so profusely about the road and pavements that screaming women dashed into the stores to escape them. By the time the downpour stopped, as suddenly as it had begun, hundreds of the small creatures had been crushed or killed, and hundreds more had hopped away into sewers, alleys and gardens.

But that shower was nothing compared to what had happened centuries beforehand in Sardinia. According to ancient Egyptian books in the library at Alexandria, a frog-fall on the island lasted three days. Frogs clogged the roads and ponds, blocked doors and poured into houses. The people could do nothing to stop the invasion. A Greek scribe wrote: "All vessels were filled with the frogs. They were found boiled and roasted with everything the Sardinians tried to eat. The people could make no use of water because it was all filled with frogs, and they could not put their feet on the ground for the heaps of frogs that were there. Those that died left a smell that drove the people out of the country."

Flakes of meat up to three inches square showered down on the American state of Kentucky from a clear blue sky in March 1876. One astonished fieldworker boldly ate some, and said they tasted like mutton. In May 1890, a shower of bright red rain drenched Messignadi, Calabria, southern Italy. The Italian Meteorological Society identified it as birds' blood.

Fish up to five inches long fell on Aberdare, South Wales, in a dense downpour in February 1859. They covered the roofs of houses and children scooped them up in the streets. Specimens sent to the British Museum were identified as minnows, and put on show at the zoo in Regent's Park, London.

A terrible thunderstorm swept the English city of Worcester in May, 1881. A donkey pulling a cart was struck dead by lightning in Whitehall, and hailstones tore leaves from trees and battered crops to the ground. In Cromer Lane, gardener John Greenhall raced to shelter in a shed, and watched astonished as the hailstorm suddenly turned into a deluge of periwinkles. They bounced off the ground and

First UFO on film

Two Swiss astronomers from Basle observed a spindle-like object, surrounded by a glowing outer ring, pass in front of the sun on August 9, 1762. The sighting corresponded with a shape seen over Mexico by hundreds of people in the 1880s. The photograph which Professor Bonilla took there through a telescope at Zacatecas observatory on August 12, 1883 is believed to be the first photograph ever taken of a UFO.

shredded the leaves of his plants, covering some parts of the ground to a depth of several inches. When the storm had passed townsfolk flocked to the area and collected the mollusks for hours. One man filled two buckets. Another picked up a huge shell and found it occupied by a hermit crab.

A rain of sprats, smelts and whiting fell on the county of Kent at Easter 1666. Some traders cheekily picked them up and sold them in Maidstone and Dartford. Hordes of yellow mice tumbled from the sky over Bergen, Norway, in 1578. Thousands fell into the sea and swam ashore like a tide. Norwegian legend has it that such showers are nature's way of replacing lemmings lost in periodic mass suicides when they rush over cliff-tops into the ocean.

What can be the real reason for these amazing falls of live creatures? The most common explanation is that they have been sucked up by whirlwinds and waterspouts elsewhere on the Earth's surface, and carried by the wind to be dumped unexpectedly where least expected. But if that were so, why are frogs not accompanied by some evidence of their environment, such as pondweed, mud or tadpoles? How can the wind select only sprats or whiting from an ocean full of different species of fish?

Charles Fort, a 19th-century American writer, believed that such living showers originated in some kind of immense

Sargasso Sea, somewhere in the atmosphere. These periodic showers replenished stocks or spread species to new parts of the globe. Sadly, nobody has yet located Fort's aerial sea.

If comets were the vehicles that brought humans to Earth, could they still be raining life down on the planet?

Deities from space

Man has found no use for the eerie, empty spaces of Peru's southern coastal plain. Nothing lives in the dry-as-dust flatland which stretches from the Pacific Ocean to the snow-capped Andes. But in 1939, two men in a plane looked down on it, and discovered complex lines and geometric patterns of astonishing precision, stretching for miles across the arid wastes. And ever since, people have been asking: was this once a landing place for aliens? Could it have been an intergalactic spaceship terminal for giant UFOs, which may have brought to Earth, in prehistoric times, the real ancestors of man?

Archaeologists and scientists have never been able to explain the sudden, dramatic evolutionary and technological leap made by *Homo sapiens* 10,000 to 15,000 years ago. There are no genetic clues to the sudden doubling in size of the human brain. In the trail pursued by the experts, there seem to be more missing links than clues.

But some say the clues are there . . . in the deserts of the world and the legends of early civilized man. They point to god-like visitors from space who passed on skills and technological knowledge to primitive man, and may even have inter-bred with him.

The amazing patterns in the Peruvian desert near the city of Nazca cover an area 37 miles long and one mile wide. The plain consists of yellow soil covered by a thin layer of stones. Each line was made by removing the surface layer of stones. The task was comparatively simple, but the un-deviating accuracy of the lines is stunning, stretching dead straight for mile after mile, passing over the horizon, cross-

The second pyramid of Khefren illustrates the majesty and the mystery surrounding the building of these mighty edifices.

ing gullies and climbing slopes. Their precision matches anything modern engineering can achieve. And they show up clearly only in very high-level aerial photographs.

Scientists who tracked them, with difficulty, on foot, could find no reason for them. They led nowhere and matched no astronomical pattern. But from far out in space, deserts would seem the most obvious place to land on a planet with as much surface water as ours. When America aimed astronauts at the Moon, it chose the lunar equivalent of our deserts. There are reasons for believing that UFOnauts may have done the same thing.

Drawn on the desert floor beside the Nazca lines and patterns are birds, spiders and fish. These too are virtually invisible at ground level. Scientists dismiss them as ancient worship objects. But that may be exactly what they were— invocations to the aerial gods to visit Earth again.

A bird was almost certainly the only other thing known to early Peruvians that could defy gravity by flying; and

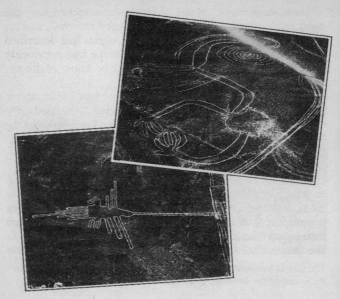

Two of the amazing patterns (top, monkey; below, hummingbird) to be seen in the Peruvian desert near the city of Nazca.

their desert bird has a tail that fans out like the blast-off trail of a rocket. The spider looks like the object we now recognize as America's spindle-legged Moon-landing craft. And the fish? They might represent the gods themselves.

On the fringes of another desert, the Sahara, lives a primitive tribe discovered just over a century ago by explorers from the West. The Dogons of Mali still worship intelligent, fish-like amphibians who, they insist, came from the sky. They called themselves the Nommos, landed in a whirling, spinning ark, and had to live in water.

They told the Dogons that they came from a tiny but heavy star called Sirius, which followed an elliptical orbit round the brightest constellation in the sky. Early explorers who listened to the tribe's story nodded their heads with amused condescension.

Then, amazingly, in the 1950s, astronomers using the most modern radio telescopes discovered the tiny, heavy, elliptical orbiting star, exactly as the Dogons had described it. So faint was it that no optical telescope had previously detected it. So how did this African tribe know of its existence?

The Dogons were not the only people visited from above during prehistory. The Sumerians called their gods the Oannes, and they, too, were amphibians. They brought the secrets of mathematics, writing and astronomy to the people of the Tigris and Euphrates valleys of Mesopotamia, long acknowledged as the birthplace of human civilization.

Berossus, a Babylonian priest, described the Oannes god as part man and part fish. He plunged into the sea "to abide all night in the deep, for he was amphiblous." In Philistine legend, the God was born from an egg which dropped from heaven into the Euphrates. Like the deities of the Dogons', the Oannes had a connection with Sirius. Their worshippers venerated the figure 50—the exact orbital period of the star, as mentioned by the Dogons.

The theory that spacemen visited our ancestors is reinforced by the art of many ancient peoples. In 1950, archaeologists uncovered the tomb of an ancient Mayan priest at Palanque, Mexico. Clearly visible on the drawings was the figure of a man in a capsule. He was surrounded by levers and machinery, and there was a fiery trail, like exhaust fumes, at the back of the craft.

In caves below the Sahara mountain range of Tassili N'Ajjer, on the present-day borders of Algeria and Libya, there is a lasting pictorial record of the daily life of a tribe forced to move on when their green oasis was drowned by the shifting sands. Drawings show water buffalo, birds and parties of armed hunters.

Among the groups are the clear figures of what we can now recognize as space travelers. They are no bigger than the hunters, but they wear space suits and helmets—round headgear with antennae.

Mysterious markings on the floor of the barren Gobi Desert in Outer Mongolia puzzled explorers and archaeologists for centuries. They were not made by any known form of fire or gunpowder. Then scientists found identical marks in the sands of the Nevada Desert in America . . . after the United States triggered its first atomic bomb test in 1944. Had a nuclear-powered UFO visited the Gobi in the long-distant past?

Across the Himalayas, Indian priests still chant the Ramayana in praise of gods who arrived on Earth in "vimanas," strange flying machines propelled by quicksilver and fierce winds. The words of the hymn relate that, "at the gods' bequest, the magnificent chariot rose up to a mountain of cloud on an enormous ray as brilliant as the sun and with a noise like a thunderstorm . . ."

Such discoveries have suggested to scientists that other marvels of ancient man may be associated with the knowledge and skills of extra-terrestrial visitors. How did the ancient Egyptians build the pyramids, and how did they discover the seemingly magical properties of the Pyramid shape? Who built the giant stone figures on lonely Easter Island, and why? What was the secret wisdom of the ancient Greek oracles?

Even some devout Christians are beginning to wonder whether their religion is based on the visits of a space race. In the Old Testament Book of Ezekiel, the Hebrew prophet records how, in the 6th century BC, he watched a weird cloud descend in the desert beside the River Chebar in Babylon. It was amber, the colour of glowing metal, and surrounded by "fire infolding itself." Four objects came out of it, each a wheel within a wheel with a ring of eyes; and out of them came man-like creatures in suits of burnished brass, with "crystal firmaments" on their heads. He might have been describing a 20th-century astronaut.

American UFO researcher Raymond E. Fowler is not alone in using such descriptive passages to determine the realities of Biblical legends. A pillar of fire guided Moses through the wilderness, and the prophet Elijah was taken to heaven in a fiery chariot. Both were clearly seen later with Jesus on the Mount of Transfiguration, glowing in contact with the "cloud" on which they stood.

In the New Testament, a pillar of fire and voices from

Space shrine

British housewife Phyllis Henderson believes Jesus Christ was a flying saucer pilot from Saturn. She turned the garage of her home at Warrington, Cheshire, into a church after joining the Aetherius Society, a movement begun by George King, who claimed he met Jesus when a UFO landed at Holdstone Down, Devon, during the early 1950s.

Phyllis, 59, and her husband Steuart, 62, received temporary planning permission to use their asbestos and brick garage as a shrine. Then neighbours complained that their services were too noisy. "The complaints are nonsense," Phyllis said. "Our church has only got seven members and they do not make a lot of noise."

"the host of heaven" told the shepherds of Christ's birth at Bethlehem; and a bright "star in the East" guided the wise men to the crib where lay the child born to a virgin. Jesus had magic, mystical powers, and ascended to heaven on a cloud. "If I have told you of earthly things and ye believe not," He told disciples, "how shall ye believe if I tell you of heavenly things?"

The "angels" of the Lord were messengers of God who came from the skies—Daniel called them "watchers"—and were allowed to intermarry and eat human food. Were they really UFO aliens who came to educate or "save" a primitive people? Was the blinding light that converted Paul on the road to Damascus a UFO bringing Jesus back to repeat His message? And will the Second Coming, with fearful sights and signs in the sky, a host of clouds and angels, really be an invasion fleet of spacemen in UFOs?

4

Encounters of the Grisly Kind

If the world's leaders and armed forces have been evasive about human casualties of attempts to challenge UFOs, they have been even more secretive about possible UFO crash landings. Yet stories persist that several flying saucers have fallen to Earth in the last 30 years—and that alien bodies have been recovered from them . . .

Mysterious wreckage in space

The wreck of a spaceship from another planet is in orbit round the Earth—and could contain the bodies of alien beings. That was the astonishing claim of Russian scientists that made front-page news in 1979.

Top Soviet astrophysicist Professor Sergei Boshich revealed that scientists first spotted wreckage floating 1,240 miles above Earth in the 1960s. They identified ten pieces of debris, two of them measuring 100 feet across, in slightly different orbits, and fed their findings into a sophisticated computer, to trace the age of the wreckage.

"We found they all originated in the same spot on the same day—December 18, 1955. Obviously there had been a powerful explosion." Man's first space rocket went up in 1957.

Another top Russian astrophysics researcher, Professor Aleksandr Kazantsev, said the two large pieces of debris gave clues about the shape and size of the craft. "We believe it was at least 200 feet long and 100 feet wide. It had small domes housing telescopes, saucer antennae for communications, and portholes.

"Its size would suggest several floors, possibly five. We believe alien bodies will still be on board."

Moscow physicist Dr. Vladimir Azhazha ruled out suggestions that the debris could be fragments of a meteor. "Meteors do not have orbits," he said. "They plummet aimlessly, hurtling erratically through space. And they do not explode spontaneously.

"All the evidence we have gathered over the past decade points to one thing—a crippled alien craft. It must hold secrets we have not even dreamed of."

Russian geologist Professor Aleksei Zolotov, a specialist in explosions, added: "The wreckage cannot be from an Earth spaceship—the explosion happened two years before we launched the world's first satellite, Sputnik I.

Mystery of the Andes

No reason was ever given for the tight security net thrown round an area near Mendoza in western Argentina in January 1964. But rumors that a UFO had lost speed and crashed, with tiny aliens in luminous suits aboard, in the foothills of the Andes, circulated for some years, and a photograph smuggled to the *Flying Saucer Review* magazine showed a mysterious cigar-shaped object, about 13 feet long, lying in rough scrubland.

"A rescue mission should be launched. The vessel, or what is left of it, should be reassembled here on Earth. The benefits to mankind could be stupendous."

Leading American scientists were at first stunned, then excited by the revelations. Dr. Henry Monteith, a physicist working on top-secret nuclear research at the Sancia Laboratories in Albuquerque, New Mexico, said the evidence warranted further investigation.

"It certainly sounds like a solid study by the Russians," he added. "It's very exciting—we could even send up a space shuttle. If it is an alien spacecraft, it would be the find of the century. It would conclusively prove the existence of intelligent life elsewhere in the universe."

Dr. Myran Malkin, director of the NASA Space Shuttle office of space technology, said: "We would consider a joint salvage attempt if the Russians approached us."

And nuclear physicist Stanton Friedman said: "If we retrieved the fragments, there's a chance we could put the pieces back together."

The British reaction was more cautious. Dr. Desmond King-Hele, a space researcher at the Royal Aircraft Establishment in Farnborough, Hants, said: "There are more than 4,000 pieces of wreckage orbiting the Earth. Each has a catalogue number to identify it. We would like to know the catalogue number of this wreck. It is possible to date wreckage after a considerable number of observations.

"Like the Americans, we would be interested to look at this if the Russians make the information available."

American physicist William Corliss recalled an article written by astronomer John Bagby in the US magazine *Icarus* in 1969—a time when government agencies had just decreed that UFOs did not exist.

He wrote that ten moonlets were orbiting the Earth after breaking off from a larger parent body. And he traced the date of the disintegration . . . December 18, 1955.

"Bagby could not explain the explosion," Corliss said. "He was only interested in proving that the objects were out there, and dismissed them as natural phenomena. It seemed the safest thing to do at that time . . ."

Other UFOs have successfully negotiated Earth's atmosphere, only to crash on to the surface of the planet, according to several American researchers. But proving their claims is virtually impossible, they say, because governments have kept all the incidents secret.

The secret of the dead aliens

It was the worst storm New Mexico had seen in years. The wind and rain raged all night, and in the middle of it all, rancher Bill Brazel heard a strange explosion. At first light he saddled his horse and rode out to make sure his sheep were all right. What he found that morning, July 3, 1947, was to make his farm world-famous—and spark off a UFO controversy that continues to this day.

His fields were covered by small beams of wood and thin sheets of metal. The wood looked like balsa and felt as light, but it was actually very hard, did not burn, and would not break. Some pieces carried strange hieroglyphics. The metal looked like tin foil, but could not be dented or bent. Then Brazel noticed a huge battered disc. As he rode closer, he saw something even more strange. There were beings, who were not human, lying beside the object. Some were alive, but they could not speak. Brazel raced back to the house and called the sheriff. He alerted nearby Roswell Army Air Field.

Intelligence chief Major Jesse Marcel led the investigating team. As ambulances carried off the burned bodies, and army trucks arrived to collect the wreckage, he threw an immediate security cordon round the fields, and told rancher Brazel not to talk about what he had seen.

New Mexico was then the hub of America's atomic, rocket, aircraft and radar research. Roswell was the home of the 509th US Air Force Bomb Group, the only combat-trained atom bombers in the world. Marcel had no idea what the crashed craft was, but he knew it should not have been over such a sensitive defence area.

On July 8, his attempts to keep the affair under wraps were jolted when the base's public information officer, Walter Haut, issued a press release without the authority of his commander, Colonel William Blanchard. It read: "The many rumours of the flying disc became reality yesterday when the intelligence office of the 509th Bomb Group gained possession of a disc through the cooperation of some local ranchers.

"The object landed at a ranch near Roswell some time last week. It was picked up at the rancher's home, inspected at Roswell Army Air Field, and loaned by Major Marcel to higher headquarters."

Wire services quickly passed the news on to papers all over the world, and the Army came under pressure to release more details. But reporters now found the story had changed. A rash of denials poured out of Roswell and Washington. A senior Air Force officer assured the public, via a Texas radio station, that the wreckage was the remains of a Rawin balloon. Newspapers were issued with a picture of him and another officer examining a balloon.

The official line soon cooled curiosity about what had happened at Roswell. But some UFO researchers were unsatisfied. Eventually Charles Berlitz, author of books on the riddle of the Bermuda Triangle, took up the trail. And in 1980 he published a book, co-written by William Moore, which accused the government of covering up the real facts—that the Roswell craft was a spaceship containing six aliens.

He quoted Grady "Barney" Barnett, a government engineer, who told friends he was one of the first to reach the site on the morning of July 3. "I was out on assignment," said Barnett, "when light reflecting off some sort of large metallic object caught my eye. It was a disc-shaped object about 25 or 30 feet across.

"While I was looking at it, some other people came up from the other direction. They told me later they were part of an archaeological team. They were looking at some dead bodies that had fallen to the ground. I think there were others in the machine that had been split open by explosion or impact. I tried to get close to see what the bodies were like. They were like humans but they were not humans.

"The heads were round, the eyes were small and they had no hair. They were quite small by our standards, and their heads were larger in proportion to their bodies.

"Their clothing seemed to be one-piece and grey in colour. You couldn't see any zippers, belts or buttons. They seemed to be all males and there were a number of them. I was close enough to touch them. While we were looking at them, a military officer drove up in a truck and took control. He told everybody the Army was taking over and to get out of the way.

"Other military personnel came up and cordoned off the area. We were told to leave and not talk to anyone about what we had seen—that it was our patriotic duty to remain silent."

Berlitz and Moore could not get the story from Barnett himself. He died in 1969. His version of the events was related by friends to whom he had talked in 1950. Rancher Brazel was also long dead, but his son Billy told how his father had found the debris.

"Father was very reluctant to talk about it," Billy said. "The military swore him to secrecy and he took that very seriously. I don't know what the craft was, but Dad once said the Army told him they had definitely established it was not anything made by us.

"He told me the occupants of the ship were still alive, but their throats had been badly burned from inhaling gases and they could not speak. They were taken to California and kept alive in respirators, but they died before anyone had worked out how to communicate with them."

Berlitz and Moore also quoted a California university physics professor, Dr. Weisberg, who said he examined the disc. "It was shaped like a turtle's back, with a cabin space inside about 15 feet wide. The interior was badly damaged. There were six occupants, and an autopsy on one revealed they resembled humans except in size.

"One body was seated at what appeared to be a control desk on which hieroglyphics were written. They were peculiar symbols. It was definitely not a known language. There was no evidence of a propellor or a motor. No one could understand how it was driven."

A Los Angeles photographer, Baron Nicholas Von Poppen, claimed he had taken pictures of the crash ship after being approached by two men from military intelligence. He said they offered him a top-secret assignment at an exceptionally high fee—but warned that if he revealed anything he saw or photographed, he would be deported.

Von Poppen, who had developed a system of photographic metallurgic analysis, said he was escorted to the Roswell air base and took hundreds of pictures, which he had to hand over at the end of each day. He described the craft as about 30 feet wide, and the cabin 20 feet across. Its floor was covered with plastic sheets on which there were symbols. There were four seats in front of a control board covered with push buttons and levers, "and in each seat, still strapped in, was a thin body, varying in height from two to four feet."

The Baron added: "The faces of all four were very white. They wore shiny black attire without pockets, closely gathered at their feet and necks. Their shoes were made of the same material and appeared very soft. Their hands were human-like though soft, like those of children. They had five digits, normal-looking joints and neatly-trimmed nails."

Berlitz and Moore said Von Poppen smuggled one negative from the craft, and locked it away in a safe place, to be opened only after his death. When he died, in 1974, aged 90, no trace of the negative was found.

The authors claim that Major Marcel was interviewed again about the Roswell incident in 1978, after he had retired to Houma, Louisiana. Asked whether the wreckage he had collected from the ranch was really a weather balloon, he said: "It was not."

He went on: "I was pretty well acquainted with everything in the air at that time, both ours and foreign. I was also acquainted with virtually every type of weather-observation or radar-tracking device being used by the military and civilians. It was something I had not seen before, and it certainly wasn't anything built by us. It most certainly wasn't any weather balloon."

In that case, why say it was? Marcel said Brigadier-General Ramey ordered the cover story "to get the Press off the Army's back." Berlitz alleged that the bodies and wreckage were secretly shipped around the country by truck and train for analysis at various scientific centres.

"We have been able to track down people who have a clear recollection of the crash, technicians who examined the alien machinery and clerks who checked the bodies into various establishments," he said. "Their stories tally too well for the whole story to be just a legend."

Berlitz believed the facts were covered up to avoid causing public panic, and for military reasons. Any nation that could work out how the disc was powered would have a massive advantage over its rivals in the missiles and space races.

Only successive incoming presidents were allowed to share the military secret. "Eisenhower, Kennedy and Johnson carried it to their graves, Nixon, Ford, Carter and Reagan have to live with it." Berlitz recalled that Jimmy Carter had promised to make government information on UFOs available to the public if elected. When the author rang the White House, he was told that reopening of UFO investigations was not warranted.

Berlitz commented: "His silence was undoubtedly prompted by the fact that he had learned something which convinced him to keep quiet about the whole issue."

UFO crashes

Have other UFO crashes been covered up? The secretive attitude of the authorities makes it impossible to confirm reports that spacecraft have fallen into the hands of earth-bound investigators.

There were strong rumours in the late 1940s that a flying saucer had come down just outside Mexico City, and that the wreckage—and the bodies of three silver-suited occupants, all only three feet tall—had been loaded onto trucks and taken to the United States for study.

Raymond E. Fowler, an authority on UFOs, particularly in New England, received what could be confirmation of the rumours when he gave a lecture on UFOs at Boston.

In his book, *UFOs: Interplanetary Visitors*, published in 1979, he said that an assistant minister at a Boston church told him he was working for the Pentagon in naval intelligence at the time.

A colleague in Mexico was assigned to help investigate an air crash. "When he arrived, the area had been roped off and personnel were loading remains of an oval object and its occupants into trucks . . . He was quickly ordered out of the area by a superior, who told him not to mention what he had seen.

Fowler traced the minister's former colleague to Belfast, Maine, where he was living in retirement. He denied all knowledge of the incident, and said his friend must have made some mistake. But the minister stood by his story. Fowler concluded that the man might be afraid to reveal his secret because he was living on a pension from the Navy.

In 1957, fishermen at Ubatuba Beach, Brazil, claimed they had seen a flying object explode and fall into the sea. They also produced fragments of ultrapure magnesium which, they said, came from the debris. The authorities were skeptical, even though they could not explain how simple fishermen could have come by magnesium which, as later tests showed, was forged by a directional casting method not even invented by 1957.

Ten years later, Raymond Fowler came across what may have been another UFO crash. He met Mr. and Mrs. Bill Marsden, who recalled driving towards Mattydale, a suburb of Syracuse, New York, during the winter of 1953–4. It was 3 A.M. on a Sunday when they came across the flashing lights of four or five police cars, and slowed, thinking there had been an accident. The road was clear, but something in a nearby field caught Mr. Marsden's eye. He told Fowler:

"I saw an object which appeared to be 20 feet in diameter and possibly 15 feet high in the centre. It had phosphorescent lights of several colours spaced over the surface. These lights were strong enough to make clearly visible quite a few men walking around the object and examining it. Some were uniformed and some were not. One had what appeared to be a large press camera with a strap and was taking pictures."

On the Monday morning, Mr. Marsden called his local newspaper to ask why it had no story of the event, then phoned the sheriff's office. He claims he was told: "Yes, we know about that, but it is a military secret and we can't discuss it." But when the newspaper talked to the sheriff's office, and to the Air Force, reporters were told that no such incident had taken place. The sheriff also denied that anyone had told Mr. Marsden about "a military secret." Mr. Marsden let the matter drop, even though he had checked the field next morning, and found indentations and tyre tracks. He knew that UFO supporters faced ridicule.

When Fowler made inquiries with the sheriff's office in 1967, he was told that the only objects which had fallen to earth during the winter of 1953–4 were a weather balloon, a wing tank from a plane, an aircraft, and a sand-filled imitation bomb dropped by mistake from another plane. None of those objects tallied with what Mr. Marsden had seen—and he stuck to his story.

Bizarre autopsies

America has recovered a total of more than 30 bodies from crashed alien craft, according to researcher Leonard Stringfield. Many have been given autopsy examinations, and all are preserved either at the Wright-Patterson Air Force base in Ohio, or at the underground Air Force complex near Colorado Springs.

Stringfield, who says that the aliens are between 3½ feet and 5 feet tall and slender, with oversized hairless heads, made his astonishing claims after talking to two doctors and six Forces personnel involved in the recovery and analysis of bodies over the last 30 years. He added that a specially trained force called the Blue Berets is on constant standby, ready to move instantly should a UFO crash.

All Stringfield's sources asked to remain anonymous, and he refused to identify them, even when questioned about his book. This is what he says they told him:

A doctor who observed an autopsy in the early 1950s described the alien corpse as just over 4 feet tall. It had a large, pear-shaped head with Mongoloid eyes recessed in the face. There were no eyelids, ear lobes, teeth or hair.

A former major and pilot in the Air Force observed strange bodies in an underground preservation chamber at Wright-Patterson during 1952 after secret Air Force instructions were sent out ordering pilots on UFO missions to shoot down strange craft.

Another USAF pilot watched three crates being delivered to Wright-Patterson in 1953. He was told they contained bodies from a flying saucer crash in Arizona. An officer said the humanoids were still alive when rescuers arrived, but died despite receiving oxygen.

An army intelligence officer viewed nine alien bodies which had been frozen at Wright-Patterson in 1966, and was told that there were 30 in various government establishments. The same man learned later that five UFOs had crashed in the Ohio, Indiana and Kentucky region between 1966 and 1968.

An Air Force sergeant and air policeman, identified only as Carl, said he was blindfolded and driven to a secret location to guard a room. When he peeped inside, he saw three small bodies, around 3 feet tall, with abnormally large heads.

A doctor who was present at an autopsy said the bodies had no digestive tracts or sex organs. And their blood was colourless.

Stringfield, whose claims were published by Mutual UFO Network, of Seguin, Texas, also tells of some aliens who got away. A colonel told him that, in 1968, he confronted strange beings who emerged from a saucer at the Nellis Air Force Base in Nevada. A beam of light paralyzed him, and he could only watch as the figures returned to their ship and took off.

Some aliens are not so expert in controlling the humans they meet. And even when their crafts land safely, they face new hazards on Earth.

Bullets that bounced off

A group of farmworkers and their wives astonished police at Hopkinsville, Kentucky, when they burst into the station at midnight. They said they had just fired shotguns and rifles at goblin-type aliens from a UFO—but that their bullets had bounced off the creatures.

The Sunday evening of August 21, 1965, turned into a nightmare for the family at Kelly, a sprawling cluster of houses seven miles from Hopkinsville. The Langfords of Sutton Farm, eight adults and three children, had returned after church services when one of the youngsters saw a brightly glowing object descend behind a barn. People on nearby farms saw it too, but the family dismissed it as a shooting star.

Then, at around 8 P.M., the dogs in the yard began bark-

Demons and demon-ships

Aggression by man against UFOs is nothing new. According to the US Air Force Academy textbook, supposed airships were treated as demon-ships in Ireland in about 1000 AD, "and in Lyons, France, 'admitted' space travellers were killed in around 840 AD"

ing. Two of the men went to the door to investigate, and saw, 50 yards away, a creature in a glowing silver suit, about 3½ feet tall, coming towards them. It had a huge head, long arms that nearly reached the ground, and large webbed hands with talons. The men grabbed a 12-gauge shotgun and a 22-calibre pistol, and fired at close range. The being was knocked over—but to the amazement of the watchers, it then jumped up again and scurried away.

The stunned family locked themselves inside, turned off all the inside lights, and put on the porch lamps. Then one of the women screamed. She looked out of the dining room window and saw a face peering in at her, with wide slit eyes behind a helmet visor. The men rushed into the room and fired, but again the creature, although hit, ran away.

A total of almost 50 rounds were blasted at the five aliens over the next 20 minutes, but none of the bullets stopped them. Radio newsman Bud Ledwith, who interviewed the family next morning, said: "Whenever one of the creatures was hit, it would float or fall over or run for cover. All the shots that struck them sounded as though they were hitting a bucket.

"The objects made no sound. The undergrowth would rustle as they went through it, but there was no sound of walking. The objects were seemingly weightless as they would float down from trees more than fall from them."

When caught by bullets or flashlights, the aliens, who seemed to approach with their hands in the air, would drop their arms and run. But they kept coming back, apparently making no attempt to enter the house, but just standing and staring at it. After 20 minutes, the creatures melted away into the night. But the scared family stayed alert for another two hours before daring to venture outside, and drive to the police. Officers who visited the farm could find no trace of the visitors.

It was an amazing story, but only Bud Ledwith seemed interested in investigating it seriously. An officer looked into it for the United States Air Force Bluebook file on UFOs, since he happened to be in the area and heard news of it on the radio. Several points of his report were later found to be erroneous. After interviewing Mrs. Lenny Langford, one of the women involved, he declared that she, her sons, their wives and some friends had attended a service of the Holy Roller Church that evening, and were "emotionally unbalanced" after working themselves into a frenzy. In fact, Mrs. Langford belonged to the Trinity Pentecostal Church, whose services are perfectly traditional.

Other investigators tried to find out whether there were any travelling circuses in the area, apparently believing that the farmers had seen escaped monkeys. Monkeys that floated? Monkeys in bullet-proof vests?

Bud Ledwith firmly believed that his witnesses were telling the truth, that they were simple folk who had no motive for trying to perpetrate a hoax. And as Dr. J. Allen Hynek, whose Centre for UFO Studies later probed the case, pointed out, they had nothing to gain from publicity, and later "suffered horribly from curiosity seekers, reporters and sensation mongers."

The case was later used as an example in the secret air

Bullet-proof

Police at Fort Beaufort, South Africa, fired shots from only eight yards when a glowing metallic object landed on June 26, 1972. But the bullets had no effect. The machine merely took off with a humming noise.

force training manual on UFOs—to show that humans can be dangerous for aliens! The textbook added: "At no time in the story did the supposed aliens shoot back, although one is left with the impression that the described creatures were having fun scaring humans."

The family decided they could no longer live at the farm and sold it.

Vigilantes on the alert

UFO fever in Virginia led to the formation of local vigilante groups in January 1965. The *Richmond Times-Despatch* quoted Sheriff John Kent of Augusta County as saying UFO reports had got "completely out of hand" and had become "dangerous to country residents."

A posse from the Brands Flat area of the Shenandoah Valley armed itself to go looking for creatures said to have landed in a UFO. But the sheriff said that even if little green men had arrived, residents "had no right to mow them down."

That was not a view shared by Attorney General Robert Button. When a Fredericksburg justice of the peace consulted him, he replied, somewhat tongue in cheek: "There is apparently no state law making it unlawful to shoot little green men who might land in the state from outer space."

In March 1966, a man driving near Bangor, Maine, did shoot at a UFO. He spotted the metallic, oval shape hovering over a field, and got out of his car to investigate, taking with him the .22 pistol from his glove compartment. When the mysterious flying object swooped towards him, scraping the tops of the bushes, the man began firing and heard bullets ricochet off metal as the craft passed overhead, before climbing out of sight at tremendous speed.

Not everyone was so unwelcoming. After a spate of local sightings, the mayor of Brewer, Maine, had a giant billboard put up inviting UFO travellers to settle down in the town.

5

Encounters of the Arresting Kind

Policemen who report strange shapes in the sky are regarded as welcome recruits by UFO enthusiasts. If such highly trained, reliable witnesses are prepared to admit the inexplicable, they argue, how can we be labelled cranks? In recent years, policemen all over the world have been converted by the evidence of their own eyes, to the possibility of aliens from other planets.

Grilling the Police

Patrolman Gene Bertrand did what any good cop would in an emergency when faced with a hostile intruder—he dropped to one knee and drew his revolver. But he was faced with no ordinary intruder. The object hurtling towards him really was out of this world.

Bertrand had been called into headquarters at Exeter, New Hampshire, to investigate the story of a kid who had come in "all shook up about some object that had chased him." Norman Muscarello had been hitch hiking home from Amesbury along Route 150 in the early hours of September 3, 1965, when a glowing red object had appeared in a field beside the road, and moved towards him.

Bertrand knew the boy. He said: "He's real tough, but something must have really scared him. He could hardly hold his cigarette and was as pale as a sheet." They drove out in the squad car to the field. They parked and sat in the car for several minutes. Nothing happened.

"I radioed the station and told them there was nothing out here," Bertrand recalled. "They asked me to take a quick walk in the field before coming back in. I must admit I felt kind of foolish walking out on private property after midnight, looking for a flying saucer.

"We walked out, me waving my flashlight back and forth, then Norman shouted, 'Look out, here it comes!' I swung around and could hardly believe what I was seeing. There was this huge dark object, as big as a barn, with red flashing lights on it. It barely cleared the trees, and it was swaying from side to side.

"Then it seemed to tilt and come right at us. I automatically dropped to one knee and drew my service revolver, but I didn't shoot. I remember suddenly thinking that that would be unwise, so I yelled at Norman to run for the cruiser. He just froze in his tracks. I had to almost drag him back.

"The thing seemed to be about 100 feet up. It was bright red with a sort of halo effect. I thought we'd be burned alive, but it gave off no heat and I didn't hear any noise from it. I did hear the horses in a nearby barn neighing and kicking in their stalls, though. Even the dogs around the area started to howl. My brain kept telling me that this doesn't happen—but it was right in front of my eyes."

Bertrand's partner, patrolman Dave Hunt, arrived while the UFO was still in sight. The three stood watching in amazement for ten more minutes. "It floated, wobbled, and did things that no plane could do," Bertrand said. "Then it just darted away over the trees towards Hampton."

As the policemen went back to their office to write their reports, Bertrand's mind went back to the woman he had met an hour earlier on Route 101. She was sitting in her parked car, "real upset" about a red glowing object that had chased her. He had sent her home without thinking much about it. Now he knew what she had seen.

Others had seen it, too. The men had not long been back in the station when a telephone operator from Hampton called. A man from a public call box claimed he had been chased by a flying saucer . . . and it was still out there. The line went dead before he could say more, and though the officers tried to locate him, they could not do so.

Air Force investigators who interrogated Bertrand and Hunt told them to keep quiet about what they had seen, so that it would not get into the newspapers. But a local newspaper reporter had already got the story.

Unable to keep it quiet, the authorities began issuing a string of curious denials. The Pentagon at first blamed the sighting on a temperature inversion that had caused "stars and planets to dance and twinkle." Officers Bertrand and Hunt protested that such a statement put their reputations as responsible policemen at risk.

Then the Pentagon claimed that Big Blast Coco, a high-altitude Strategic Air Command exercise, was responsible. The town of Exeter was within the traffic pattern used, said the war chiefs, adding: "During their approach the aircraft would have been displaying standard position lights, anti-collision lights and possibly over-wing and landing lights.''

But Bertrand had an answer to that one, too. He wrote another protest letter, saying: ''Since I was in the Air Force for four years engaged in refuelling operations with all kinds of military aircraft, it was impossible to mistake what we saw for any kind of military operation . . . Immediately, after the object disappeared we did see what probably was a B-47 at high altitude, but it bore no relation at all to the object we saw.''

The two officers also pointed out that they saw the UFO at 3 A.M., nearly an hour after the exercise ended.

Grudgingly, the Air Force gave way—but only a little. ''The early sightings . . . are attributed to aircraft from Operation Big Blast Coco,'' their final statement said. ''The subsequent observations by officers Bertrand and Hunt occurring after 2 A.M. are regarded as unidentified.''

Even such a small admission was a huge advance for UFO believers frustrated by years of officialdom's stubborn refusal to acknowledge that there could be such things.

The following March, Exeter was again visited by a UFO. One Sunday night, a police sergeant checking doors in the town around 10 P.M. saw a fast-moving white light falling to the west. He climbed a hill to get a better view, and saw what looked like a lighted egg with rotating red, white, blue and green lights underneath it, moving slowly back and forward. Then it plunged quickly down to hover over power lines.

The sergeant radioed headquarters, and a lieutenant arrived, carrying binoculars. He had always been skeptical about UFOs, despite the sightings the previous September by his own men. Now, as he peered at the egg-shaped object with a bright white dome on top, he was converted. Officer Bertrand and a newspaperman also saw the UFO. But this time nobody made a fuss about it. The town was clearly determined to live down the notoriety aroused by the earlier sightings.

No pictures please

Police chief Jeff Greenhaw lost both his wife and his job because of what he claims he saw on the night of October 17, 1963. But he stuck to his story.

It was just after 10 P.M. when he took the call at his home in Falkville, Alabama. A woman said she had seen a UFO with flashing lights land in a field west of town. Greenhaw, 26, was off duty at the time, but decided to investigate anyway. He took his camera.

As he drove up a gravel road towards the remote landing site, he saw a figure in the middle of the track. It was about the size of a large human, but was clad in a silvery suit that looked like tin foil. Antennae seemed to sprout from its head. As it moved towards him, he shot four flash pictures, then turned on the revolving light on top of his car. The figure turned and ran, "faster than any human I ever saw."

Greenhaw agreed to publish his pictures, which showed the blurred shape of an astronaut-type figure. But within four weeks, he was to regret it. His wife left, unable to cope with the publicity and "side effects." Greenhaw's car engine blew up, then a caravan he owned went up in flames. Finally, on November 15, he was asked to quit his job.

Whether he saw an alien or a hoax invented by someone with a grudge was never established. Many other people reported odd lights that night, but despite their evidence, Greenhaw's superiors felt that his credibility had diminished.

In pursuit of the unknown

The black Chevrolet shot past the courthouse at Socorro, New Mexico, far faster than it should have done. Patrolman Lonnie Zamora gunned the engine of his patrol car into action, and swung out into Old Rodeo Street in pursuit. He

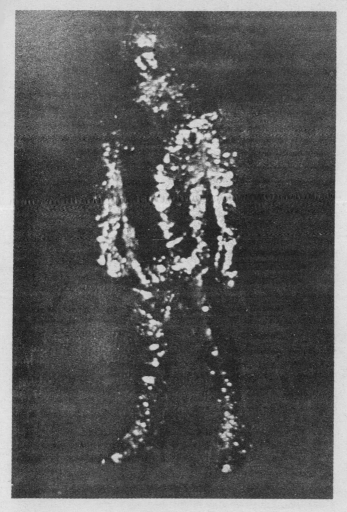

This UFO entity was photographed by Police Chief Jeff Greenhaw at Falkville, Alabama on October 17, 1973.

noted the time for his report—it was 5.45 on April 24, 1964. Zamora would never catch the speeder, but he would remember that day for the rest of his life.

As he accelerated out of town, he noticed a flame in the sky, a mile or so to the south-west. He also heard a roar. The noise came from the direction of a dynamite storage shack. Had it blown up? He decided to abandon the chase and investigate.

He swerved off the road and on to a rough gravel track. The tapered blue and orange flame seemed to be descending against the setting sun. He lost sight of it as he struggled to steer the car up a small hill. Three times he had to reverse and try another route as gravel and rock spun the wheels.

At the top of the hill, Zamora looked round for the shack. Then a shiny object 150 yards away caught his eye. "It looked at first like a car turned upside down," he recalled. "I thought some kids might have turned it over. I saw two people in white coveralls very close to the object. One seemed to turn and look straight at my car. He seemed startled, to quickly jump somewhat."

The officer began manoeuvering his car closer, with the idea of giving help. When he next looked at the object, the two figures—small adults or children—had vanished. The oval shape was whitish, like aluminium. He stopped the car, and radioed to HQ that he was leaving to investigate a possible accident.

As he put down his microphone, Zamora heard two or three loud thumps, "like someone hammering or shutting a door hard." Then the roar began, growing louder and increasing in frequency. "It was nothing like a jet," the policeman told investigators. "I know what jets sound like."

Now he saw the blue and orange flame again, and the object was going straight up into the air. He noted that it was oval and smooth, and saw no doors or windows, only a red insignia drawing, about 30 inches wide. As the roar increased, Zamora turned and ran—"I thought the thing was going to blow up."

He ran past his own car, stumbling as his leg struck the back bumper, and kept going, glancing over his shoulder a couple of times to see what was happening. The craft was still rising slowly from the deserted gully where it had landed. The officer dived over the top of a ridge and spread himself on the ground, covering his head with his arms.

As the roar stopped, he gingerly peeped over the hilltop. The object was speeding away towards the south-west, about 10 to 15 feet above the ground. Then it suddenly lifted higher into the sky and flew off rapidly, without sound or smoke, finally disappearing behind nearby mountains. Zamora radioed his story in to the duty desk sergeant, and a second squad car sped to the scene. The reinforcements noted ''landing marks'' about 2 to 3 inches deep in the hard-packed, sandy surface. Greasewood bushes and grass around them were scorched and smoldering,

Air Force investigators arrived a few days later, intent on finding some natural explanation for what patrolman Zamora had seen. They tried hard to establish that some man-made craft had been in the area, but without success. Colleagues described Zamora as a solid, well-liked citizen, a down-to-earth character of integrity. Cynics said that residents living near the site had seen and heard nothing; that the scorch marks could have been caused by a cigarette lighter; that the ''landing marks'' could have been created with a small shovel, or by moving boulders; that the land was owned by the town's mayor, who would welcome the publicity and tourists attracted by a UFO report.

Other investigators, however, were forced to admit that Zamora had probably seen some real phenomenon of undetermined origin. One of them was Dr. J. Allen Hynek, who, talking later of the scorn some critics poured on UFO reports, said: ''It is paradoxical that the testimony of policemen, which in some cases might be sufficient to send a man to the electric chair, is in instances like this often totally disregarded.''

Similar sightings, of a white, aluminium-like oval shape, were reported right across the United States that spring. It was seen at La Madera, New Mexico, Helena, Montana, and Newark, New Jersey. The last witness also reported seeing curious child-size creatures beside the grounded craft.

The acrobatic disc

Detective Sergeant Norman Collinson watched a disc-like object perform 90-degree turns at incredible speed above the town of Bury, Lancashire, in April, 1976. The officer, who later became an inspector, said: "After a while it streaked away at an even higher speed, reaching the horizon in around two seconds."

Cops in confusion

A woman police officer and a male colleague spotted a long, cigar-shaped object hovering 500 feet above the select residential district of Rickmansworth, Hertfordshire, at 3:25 on November 29, 1979. It was brilliantly lit along its entire length, and had red lights above and below it. It made no sound. WPC Anne Louise Brown, 21, admitted later: "I was scared stiff when it was above our car. I don't know what it was, but it was definitely too big and too bright to be a plane or a star. I told my colleague he must be crackers to report it back. I was sure people would think we were potty."

Minutes later, two other officers, both men, saw the same shape above nearby Chorley Wood, and gave chase in their Panda car after alerting HQ. It flew quietly out of sight, but two hours later they spotted it again.

Hertfordshire police checked with West Drayton air traffic control, and confirmed that no planes were in the area. Inspector George Freakes said: "This is being treated seriously. We are convinced the officers saw something—they are very genuine types—but as yet no one can explain exactly what it was."

Patrolmen from several forces gave chase when a UFO was spotted over Will County, Illinois, south of Chicago, in the pre-dawn darkness of November 25, 1980. And the mysterious shape led them a merry dance.

Sheriff's deputies Lieutenant Karl Sicinski and Sergeant Jay Mau were first to see the UFO, about 1,500 feet up and two miles away. It drifted south, shot off east, then turned north, and finally ended up to the south-east of them.

"It was faster than any plane I ever saw," said Sicinski, who flew fighter jets during his days in the US Navy. "I've never seen any aircraft that can manoeuver as tightly as this object did. It was huge and very bright. It was shaped like a teardrop lying on its side and had a pinkish-whitish cast to it."

Policemen in neighbouring towns Frankfort, New Lenox and Mokena overheard Sicinski radio his report to HQ, and saw the shape he mentioned. Frankfort patrolman Sam Cucci was driving west towards the UFO when he spotted it rising, getting brighter, then dimming its lights.

"Suddenly, I lost sight of it," he recalled. "I asked two other squad cars where it was and they said, 'It's behind you.' So I whipped the squad car round to the east and, with the two other units, gave chase at about 60 mph. I put on my spotlight, but the UFO veered away and then just dissipated, like it was a light and someone shut it off."

In New Lenox, officers Carl Bachman and Charles Proper watched the UFO zigzag across the sky for 20 minutes. "I won't forget that night," said Bachman. "There is some-

---

Column of light

Inspector Desmond Condon was among the many people who reported a column of light, stretching almost 3,000 feet, above Earlsfield, south-west London, in November 1977. "It was a perfect pillar," he said. "It glowed with a bluish haze and stayed motionless for about 30 minutes. I've never seen anything like it."

thing out there we don't know about." Proper said: "It was a bright light, and all of a sudden it just went straight up and disappeared. In a matter of just one or two seconds it was out of sight."

Mokena patrolman Tom Donegan, who also saw the UFO, said: "It makes you wonder who's out there watching us."

In March 1981 came news of a bizarre encounter involving a chief of police. Miguel Costa, in charge of the force at Melo, Uruguay, was driving with his wife Carmen and friends Armando and Maria Pena along a gravel road near Tacuarembo when a huge shape, gleaming with orange and yellow lights, loomed out of the early morning darkness in front of them.

Costa stopped the car, and, on impulse, flashed the headlights. "All of a sudden the UFO hesitated, then zigzagged up and back as if answering our call," the police chief reported.

"As soon as we started out again, it was there following us. I again stopped the car and flashed my lights. Again the UFO wavered in reply. We drove on once more on the twisting road and the UFO stayed with us, always about half-a-mile away. This went on for almost 30 miles. That's when the strangest thing of all occurred.

"We were all glued to the windows watching as the disc suddenly shot towards the ground as if it was going to crash. It stopped 50 to 100 yards from the earth, and we could clearly see its round, dome-like shape with a large flat plate underneath. There was a slight ring of cloud around the dome. The top was reddish but the bottom was a brilliant glowing white."

Feeling somehow menaced by the craft's new, lower flight path, Costa turned the car round and headed back towards Tacuarembo, the nearest town. The blazing light of the UFO remained constant in the rear window. Costa pulled over and parked under some trees.

"We walked over to a little clearing and looked up," the policeman said. "A second disc was moving some distance behind the first. They never touched, but they seemed to be travelling together. They moved up and down and clouds started to form.

"They passed over the top of the clouds and lit them up like a halo. Then they faded, getting smaller and smaller until finally they had gone. It was dawn. They had been over us for 90 minutes. We looked at each other without speaking. We still couldn't believe what we had seen."

Chief Costa paused, then added: "I never believed in UFOs before, but I realize now that I have seen something special and unreal."

Follow that UFO!

Five policemen saw a multicoloured flying object hovering above the town of Dumfries, Scotland, late in 1979. Two of them later described the sighting at a press conference.

The officers were called in after a flood of calls from people going home after the pubs shut. They saw the huge shape for about 20 minutes before it streaked away over nearby hills.

Sergeant Bill McDavid, 39, said he drove to within a mile of the thing. It was larger than any aircraft and seemed to be 500 feet up. Its shape was like that of an airship, with five or six white lights shining from separate compartments.

PC James Smith said: "I never believed in UFO's up to now. It was raining at the time and the cloud base was very low. The shape remained stationary for 20 minutes then vanished over the hills to the west."

Mary Blyth, 22, and her sister Vicky, 19, were just two of the people who rang the police after they spotted the UFO. "The lights appeared from nowhere," said Mary. "We just stood there and stared at it in amazement."

Glasgow weather centre said it was not unknown for low clouds to reflect bright lights from Earth, but a spokesman added: "If light from the ground is reflected, it is usually just a yellowish glare. I have never heard of a cluster of coloured lights in the way that has been described. I have no explanation as to what these people really saw.''

Two patrolmen in Minnesota spotted a glowing white ball after being called out by Farmington housewife and computer programmer Karen Anondson in September, 1979. ''It was definitely a UFO,'' said patrolman Dan Siebenaler, of the Farmington Force. ''I am familiar with what is in the night sky, and that thing did not belong there.'' Steve Kurtz, an officer from neighbouring Apple Valley police, said: ''It was something unexplainable, I've never seen anything like it before.'' Mrs. Anondson, 32, said she had seen the ball at least nine times as she drove home from work. ''It's become a normal thing,'' she said. ''I look for it when I come out of the office.''

A few months earlier, a Minnesota deputy sheriff reported a frightening encounter with a UFO. Val Johnson was driving his patrol car on a lonely road near Warren when he saw a bright light about 2½ miles away. ''I drove towards it to find out what it was,'' he recalled. ''After I'd gone about a mile, the light rushed towards me. It was a brilliant light, so brilliant it was almost painful.

''I remember the brakes locking when I applied them, and I remember the sound of breaking glass. Then I lost consciousness for about 30 minutes. When I came too, I radioed for help.''

Officers who examined the car found that both the windshield and a headlight had been broken, and the top of the hood was dented. Even more curious was the fact that the two spring-loaded whip antennae on the roof had been bent at an angle of 90 degrees. ''The damage to the hood, windshield and headlight might have been caused by stones or rocks,'' said UFO researcher Allen Hendry. ''But there's no explaining how the antennae, which are extremely flexible, got to be bent that way.''

Doctors who checked the deputy sheriff after his ordeal had to treat burns round his eyes. They were of the kind welders suffer when they fail to use protective masks.

A dozen policemen in Tennessee watched a UFO for two hours in February 1980. It amazed the people of three towns in two counties with its aerial antics, hovering, then shooting off at impossible speeds and incredible angles.

Deputy sheriff Franklin Morris, from Winchester, first heard about the strange sight over his radio, and raced to a hill to get a good view of it. "At first I thought it might be a plane, but there was no noise at all, no engine, no rocket. It hovered a while, three or four minutes. Then it decided to take off, and moved so fast you could hardly watch it. I've seen some pretty fast jets in my time, but never anything like this."

Winchester patrolmen Milton Yates and Gerald Glasner saw bright red and white lights coming towards them as they drove on the east side of town. "It was coming towards us and it stopped, sat two or three minutes, then shot off at 500 or 600 mph," said Sergeant Yates "The way it took off it couldn't have been an aircraft. It had no moving lights, no noise, just those flashing lights, and it went round in circles. I feel real sure it was a UFO."

Officer Glasner added: "It was not like anything we've got here on Earth. The speed, maneouverability, those flashing lights, the silence." Officers from nearby Monteagle and Cowan also watched the UFO in amazement. When they checked with the National Weather Service station at Nashville, officials could offer no alternative natural explanation.

Two Michigan policemen chased a multicoloured, shapeless craft for more than 26 miles in March 1980 after picking it up in the sky over Gladstone. "It was glowing orange, with a green light in the rear, red lights top and bottom,

---

Forest phantom

Two policemen responded to a 999 call at Hainault Forest, Essex, early one May morning in 1977, and spotted a tent-like object glowing red through the trees. They watched it "pulsing" for three minutes, then it dissolved into the darkness.

> **Arrest that saucer!**
>
> **PC Chris Bazire and WPC Vivienne White spotted a flying saucer 500 to 700 feet above Salisbury Plain, Wiltshire, in November 1977. "It was oblong with a domed top and flat bottom," they reported. "It was travelling very slowly at first, then shot off at tremendous speed, leaving a vapour trail."**

and a blinking white light at the front," said patrolman David Mariin, 26.

The men radioed for assistance as they followed the lights for nearly an hour through winding roads and dense forest. Two more police units joined the chase, and the four officers in the other cars all saw the object above the trees as it darted from side to side, leading them on, then vanishing at astonishing speed.

"I was rather skeptical about UFOs before this," said Mariin's partner, Mark Hager, 22. "But this made a believer out of me." The men checked with nearby K. I. Sawyer Air Force base, but were told nothing unusual had been spotted on the radar. "No one there seemed very interested," Mariin said. "It was almost as if they didn't want the public to know."

Three policemen were among hundreds who saw a gigantic bullet-shaped object which cruised through the night sky above Kansas and northern Missouri for four hours on November 18, 1980. Adair County deputy sheriff Charles Cooper and Missouri highway patrolman Bob Lober were amazed when it flew backward without turning round. And patrolman Mike Leavene said: "I've never seen anything like it before."

People in at least 22 towns reported seeing the UFO as it crisscrossed the two states. Don Leslie, a 42-year-old welder from Milan, Missouri, said: "It was at least as big as a football field." Roger Bennett, 40, of Huntsville, Missouri, said: "It was so big it would make a B-52 bomber look like a Piper Cub."

He added: "It was like a big fat cigar, travelling very high from east to west. You could hear a faint rumbling when it was overhead. Just before it disappeared above some clouds it ejected about six smaller objects in a fan-shaped burst. They sped off in different directions."

Truck driver Randy Hayes, 26, also saw the UFO drop its "satellites." He said: "They were round and had a bluish glow. The mother ship was so big, it blocked out a lot of stars."

In Trenton, Missouri, photographic student Rick Hull, 19, took a picture of a triangle of lights, which looked like a boomerang. He said the object seemed to make a banking movement, thus revealing lights from the "windows of a cockpit." Music teacher Buddy Hannaford and his wife Karla both saw lights "as if from the cabin of a plane." Karla, who watched through binoculars, said: "The thing was delta- or triangle-shaped, with two white lights and a red beacon on the bottom. It passed right over our house."

The burning cross

Two Devon policemen hit the headlines in 1967 when they chased bright lights in the shape of a pulsating cross. Constables Roger Willey and Clifford Waycott spotted the glowing UFO over Hatherleigh at 4 A.M. on October 24 while on routine patrol in their car, and pursued it for some distance along narrow lanes before it shot off across fields. Critics said the shape could have been aircraft refueling in mid-air from a tanker plane, which would explain the cross-like effect, and the British Defence Ministry confirmed that such exercises were going on in the area. But they had been completed by 9 P.M. the previous evening.

The object was picked up on radar at the Federal Aviation Administration station north of Kirksville, Missouri. Technician Franklin West said: ''It went through the area four or five times. I estimated the speed at about 45 mph. I'm not saying it was a flying saucer. I am saying it was an unidentified flying object, because I couldn't identify it.''

6

Encounters of the Concentrated Kind

UFOs have been reported over almost every country in the world. But certain spots on the globe seem to get far more than their fair share of sightings. Britain, Brazil, America and Europe all have areas where the locals have strange stories to tell. So do UFOs home in on specific targets? And, if so, why?

The Warminster visitations

The Thing that terrorised the Salisbury Plain

Warminster was for centuries just a quiet, unremarkable country town on the edge of Salisbury Plain. Little happened to disturb the day-to-day routine of its 14,000 inhabitants. Then, early on Christmas Day, 1964, a strange drone jolted postmaster Roger Rump from his sleep at his home in Hillwood Lane. He heard a violent rattle, like tiles being ripped off his roof. The Thing had arrived.

Two weeks later, his neighbours, Mr. and Mrs. Bill Marson, were woken three times in one night by the sound of "coal being tipped down our outside wall." Then Mrs. Rachel Attwell, wife of an RAF pilot, was roused by a curious noise at 4 A.M. She looked out of her bedroom window in Beacon View and saw a cigar-shaped, glowing object hovering in the sky, bigger and brighter than any star. Another housewife who spotted it, Mrs. Kathleen Penton, described the craft as "something like a railway carriage flying upside down, with all the windows lit up."

Soon more and more people were scanning the heavens above Wiltshire. On June 2, a total of 17 people—including Mrs. Patricia Phillips, wife of the vicar of Heytesbury, and three of her children—watched the cigar-shaped Thing for 20 minutes in the late evening. By the end of 1965, three people had even taken pictures of it. And strange things were starting to happen.

A flock of pigeons mysteriously fell from the sky. Naturalist David Holton examined the bodies, and declared that the birds had been killed by soundwaves not known on Earth. Then a farmer found that several acres he had left fallow were now a mass of weeds—silvery thistles of a type considered virtually extinct in England since 1918. And in Warminster itself, the East Street garden of Harold and Dora Horlock became another horticultural attraction when ordinary thistles that normally grew to only 5 ft. 6 in. soared to nearly 12 ft. tall.

The curious freaks of nature brought newspaper reporters and television teams flocking to the town. And as news of the UFO sightings spread, observers from all over Britain turned Warminster into a Mecca. They were not disappointed. Few months went by without a sighting. The months turned to years, and the area of activity was pinpointed as a triangle roughly bordered by Warminster, Winchester in Hampshire, and Glastonbury in Somerset. Local folk became used to their curious visitors. Mysterious lights in the sky, agitated animals, stalling cars and electrical equipment going haywire became almost commonplace. Then, in November 1976, the Thing made contact with the humans.

Mrs. Joyce Bowles, 42, was out driving in the countryside near her Winchester home with a family friend, retired farm manager Ted Pratt, 58. Suddenly she felt the car "seem to take to the air" before it stopped completely. The two stared into the inky darkness of the lonely lane. Then Mrs. Bowles began screaming in terror. A huge pink-eyed creature was peering at them through the windscreen.

"Those eyes were horrible, as bright as the sun," she recalled. "They belonged to a figure who looked like a well-built man in a silvery boiler-suit. There was a sound like a kettle whistling just before we saw him. After examining us, he returned to a glowing, cigar-shaped craft which was hovering in a field only yards from us. We could see three people inside it. When the figure got back in, the craft swiftly disappeared."

Mr. Pratt, who lived at Nether Wallop, Stockbridge, Hants, said: "I was frightened when the car began to shudder, but when the creature looked at me I suddenly felt very calm. I suppose he must have given me some power to look after Mrs. Bowles, because she was in a dreadful state. It was an unnerving experience."

It was only the first of four close encounters of the third kind for Mrs. Bowles. Weeks later, she was again driving in the country with Mr. Pratt when they heard the same shrill whistling, and the car began to rock.

"Suddenly we were both inside this machine," Mrs. Bowles recalled. "One of the spacemen standing a few feet from me was the same man I saw the first time. Lights were blinking and flashing everywhere. The man told us this was his field, whatever that meant. One of his colleagues pulled out a paper which had all sorts of lines on it. In the middle was a circle with rings round it.

"The men all had high jackboots with pointed toes. The boots were luminous, like their silvery suits. In the middle of their belts was something like a glittering stone, and the man next to me kept pressing his stone or touching it. Ted believed it was something to do with receiving messages.

"It all ended quite suddenly. We just seemed to come round, and found ourselves back in the car, stationary. By a river, completely lost. A powerful beam of light filled the car, then gradually seemed to shrink away into the sky."

A month later, on March 7, Mrs. Bowles could guess what was coming next when her car again faltered in a dark country lane. But this time she was with Ann Strickland, an old friend who had been very dubious about her earlier stories of meeting spacemen.

"We both got out of the car, then we saw this oval shape, glowing luminously, making a humming sound," Mrs. Bowles said. "A man got out and walked towards me, holding out his hands. He came right up to me and took my hand. He eyed Ann up and down. She was terrified. So was I, but I didn't show it.

"The man started to speak in a foreign language. Then he switched to broken English. I said 'Yes', but I wasn't sure what he'd said. Then he said something to me which I understood. But I can't tell anyone what it was. I wouldn't dare.

"The man looked like a spaceman I had seen in the area before, but his hair was rather longer. It fell in front of his shoulders like a woman's. I could see what looked like buckles on the bottom of his legs, and he was wearing something like gaiters. His touch was warm, like a human being.

"Once he had told me what he had to say, he turned round and walked back to the Thing. We watched it rise in the air and slip away into the sky with a high-pitched hum. Ann and I had been on our way to visit friends, but we went straight back to my home in Winchester."

Mrs. Strickland, 65, said: "I didn't hear what the man said to Joyce and she refuses point-blank to tell me because of a promise she made to him. My mind went blank. I was so surprised and shocked to see him there, and frightened. I've never had such an experience before. At my age I'm a bit too old to have shocks like that."

Mrs. Bowles's health suffered after this encounter. She had a chest infection, then her hands swelled and she had to remove her wedding ring because the area around it was raw.

There was still one more meeting to come, this time in broad daylight. In June 1977 Ted Pratt was again the passenger when the car was seized, as if by a mysterious force, and deposited in a lane off the Petersfield Road out of Winchester. Two men got out of a silver machine hovering 70 feet away and walked towards them. They were different from the figures Mr. Pratt had encountered before.

"These had sandy hair and were wearing dull metallic suits," he said. "They said something that sounded like trying to help mankind—something about war. They held out their hands and took our hands. I was very frightened. They were making signals with their hands that I could not understand. They said they were scared man would destroy himself, and pollute the atmosphere.

"Then they just said goodbye and returned to their spacecraft. It soared away into the sky and disappeared out of sight. We stood there totally shaken. I suppose we had been with those people for about ten minutes."

Mrs. Bowles said: "Something like a silver disc was pressed in my right hand. Later a peculiar white mark appeared on my palm. They said they would be back, but I don't want any more. I feel like a marked person. It's no good talking to anyone about it. People don't believe me."

But many people did believe Mrs. Bowles—people who had met what they, too, believed to be beings from outer space.

Tough German parachutist Willy Gehlen had seen many

years service with the French Foreign Legion. He liked to keep in practice, and in mid-September 1976 he was on his way from home at Bishops Castle, Shropshire, to the Army Parachute Centre at Netheravon, near Salisbury, when he decided to stop for the night and sleep in his estate car. After searching in vain for a camping site, he pulled in beside a farm gate near Upton Scudamore, a village two miles from Warminster on the Westbury road.

He fell asleep after locking all the doors, but woke shivering in the early hours to find the hatch-door at the back of the vehicle wide open. He slammed it shut, turned the key, and curled up again in his blankets. The same thing happened.

"Normally I sleep very lightly and hear the slightest sound," he said. "But I had heard no one open that door. Feeling uneasy and a little unsettled, I decided against more sleep and started to prepare a cup of coffee on my camping stove. It was 3 A.M."

Then, above the sound of a distant train, Gehlen heard a strange humming sound, "like a swarm of bees in flight," and became aware of a figure standing behind the farm gate 10 yards away. "The sheer size of this person made me wonder—he was almost 7 feet tall—but I was not frightened. I assumed it was the farmer guarding his animals against rustlers, and explained that I was only camping there for one night. There was no answer. Instead he shone a sort of square-shaped torch at me from his chest. The light was dark orange, and I thought he needed some new batteries.

"I got on with making my coffee, and when I looked up a minute or so later, he had gone. Then I heard the humming noise again, and saw a large shape lift off the ground. There was a pink, pulsating glow underneath it, and I watched it disappear across the field. It lifted to about 45 degrees above the ground, but I assumed the farmer was towing something up a hill. It was only after it became light that I realized there was no hill."

The baffled ex-airman discussed the incident with pals in his local pub when he got home. When he took their advice, and consulted a UFOlogist, he realised that he might have met an alien.

Londoners Steve Evans and Roy Fisher have made frequent special trips to the Warminster area since 1971 to try to spot UFOs. They claim to have seen at least 30, and to have had two even closer encounters.

The first happened as they gazed at the sky from the top of Cradle Hill, one of several vantage points around the town. "A forcefield seemed to move through the grass like a snake, crackling furiously like static electricity," Evans said. "It came straight for Roy's feet, then veered suddenly to the right. Sheep in the field were going frantic. When daylight came, we found flattened grass, as though something had landed."

That same weekend, the two friends had an unnerving experience at the top of nearby Starr Hill. Evans said: "We got the distinct feeling we were being watched. I glanced over my shoulder and saw a figure in a sort of white boiler suit, with a white hat, running towards a clump of bushes. I started to chase him. I was making a row myself, crashing through the bracken, but I swear he wasn't making any noise at all. After a while he slowed down, looked back for a second, then disappeared into the bushes."

Fisher added: "When Steve ran, I followed instinctively, even though I didn't know what he was after. I reached the bushes after he did, then someone brushed up against me and ran away. I didn't see or hear anything, but it wasn't imagination. He felt as solid as a man of average size and weight."

Sally Pike and her husband Neil also saw something strange on Starr Hill. They were among a group of eight UFO watchers, and had spotted two unidentified, high-flying objects when they all felt the air grow suddenly warmer.

Sally went on: "These two figures appeared. They were about 7 feet tall, and it was as if they were made out of smoke. We could see their outlines down to their waists, then they gradually started to fade away.

"When Neil approached them, he just seemed to blend in with them. He couldn't see them when he got close, but we watched him walk straight through the figures and out the other side. The figures remained in the same place for about half-an-hour, then disappeared.''

Ken Rogers was so intrigued by the mystery of the Warminster Thing that he moved to the town from London to study the evidence at first hand. One night he came across an enormous white object blocking a track down Cradle Hill.

"It was a classic saucer design, perfectly outlined," he recalled. "As I got closer, I got very hot and my hands started perspiring heavily. I walked on right through it, whatever it was. It seemed like fog, only you could see every detail absolutely clearly."

Rogers, a director of the British UFO Society, added: "I think UFOs are extra-terrestrial forces. It is the most likely explanation for them. Remember, 50 years ago people were laughing hysterically at the notion of man going to the Moon. I believe it would only take a race maybe 50 years more advanced than us to make visits of this kind feasible. I don't think the UFOs mean us any harm, so I'm not frightened at all. I believe they are studying our progress.''

Tapping the energy

Why did the Thing choose Warminster? That is the question that has baffled UFO experts. The town is close to a large army base, and large areas of nearby Salisbury Plain are used by the armed forces for exercises. Many so-called UFO sightings over the years have been traced to flares or equipment used by the Services. But many remain inexplicable. And a Territorial Army commander is among those who have reported the enigmatic cigar-shaped flying saucer. It stalled his car in January 1979.

UFOs have, in fact, often been spotted near military bases all over the world. The US Defense Department admitted in secret papers that unexplained aerial activity over missile sites and nuclear silos gave cause for concern during 1975. But the number of separate sightings at Warminster, over

Glastonbury Tor, Somerset, south-west England.

so many years, is unique. And if UFOs, as many people believe, are manned by intelligent beings, they would know that there are far more important military targets on Earth than Salisbury Plain.

Two other theories for the sightings, which have averaged two a week since 1964, have been put forward. Just outside the Warminster Triangle lies Stonehenge, thought by many to be an ancient ''computer'' for astronomers. And the town of Warminster itself lies at the crossroads of 13 ley lines, the mysterious straight lines formed by monuments, graves, burial grounds, stone crosses and other ancient holy places.

Several scientists and historians believe the ley line network had strange powers that tapped the energy of the Earth centuries ago, and that Stonehenge was a powerhouse for this energy. Man has lost the ability to use it, though some people claim to receive electric shocks from some of the ancient stones. Could it be that aliens can tap the energy, or are attracted to Earth because of it? Could it even be that they guided the early Britons to create the lines during earlier visits to Earth?

Other UFOlogists look to the West Country to account for the concentration of activity over southern England. The historic town of Glastonbury forms one outer limit of the Warminster Triangle. Legend says that the Holy Grail— the cup from which Jesus Christ drank at the Last Supper— was brought to Britain by Joseph of Arimethea, and buried at Glastonbury Tor in about AD 60. Many people who have spotted the bright lights in the sky over Warminster sincerely believe that they herald the Second Coming.

Brazilian balls of fire

For some unknown reason, Brazil seems to get more than its fair share of UFOs. They are seen frequently, coming from both the sea and the sky. On June 27, 1970, Mrs. Maria Machado looked from the window of her Rio de Janeiro home as she prepared lunch, and saw a metallic grey disc with a transparent dome apparently sailing on the ocean. Two figures in shiny clothes were moving around on the deck. Her husband, four daughters and a policeman also saw the strange craft. After 40 minutes, it skimmed along the surface and took off, leaving behind a white hoop-like object which floated out to sea.

On September 12, 1971, typewriter mechanic Paulo Silveira claimed that two figures in one-piece blue suits dragged him inside a shining disc. He told the authorities he was driving home at Itaperuna, north of Rio, when the disc blocked the road. A luminous beam shot out and his car engine died, then his own energy drained away. He heard an engine start as the two aliens, about the size of ten-year-old children, carried him aboard; then he went into a coma. He came round to find them carrying him out again. They laid him beside his car, returned to their craft, and took off.

Another motorist found him dazed, blinded and disoriented, and drove him to hospital. He had lost three hours of his life.

In January 1981, farmer Domingos Monteiro Brito claimed that he met two strange beings when a grey, glowing flying saucer landed at dawn on his land at Camaracu Island. The aliens, who resembled humans, asked him a string of questions in his own language—how many people lived in his village, were there any large uninhabited areas nearby—but he was too paralyzed with fear to remember if he answered. The craft took off again, but the beings told him they would be back.

Early in 1980, the 30,000 residents of Tres Coroas, south of Rio, experienced one of the strangest concentrations of UFOs ever recorded. Over 20 days, balls of fire chased cars, flames erupted without burning anything, and scores of strange shapes zoomed through or over the city.

Bicycle-shop owner Joao Jose de Nascimento was driving home late at night when a fire-like object appeared beside his car, apparently following him. He said: "It was strange and I was afraid. I felt it was trying to capture me." When he got home, his son Vicente told him he had seen another UFO—an onion shape revolving in the sky, with lights which switched from green to orange to blue. Estate agent Roberto Francisco Santana said he saw the shadow of a saucer travelling very fast as he drove through town with his wife and children. Then he spotted two more saucers flying over city buildings. "While I was looking up, I smashed into a car in front of me," he said. "The things we saw were very frightening."

Military police commander Antonio das Gacas Santos said he raced to a neighbour's home when he noted that the back garden was curiously illuminated. "I saw very clearly a creature about the height of a human being with its arms extended. I couldn't see any physical details, but I heard a low whining noise, like a puppy. My neighbour touched the creature, then fell back shocked. I was afraid, but it wasn't a normal fear. I still get goose-bumps thinking about it."

Rio psychiatrist Dr. Gloria Machado was astonished by

what she saw when she and her husband Mario, president of the Brazilian Association of Parapsychology, arrived in the city. "There was a fire which didn't burn anything, and flashes of light which exploded in the tree tops," she said. "Indoors I saw a box of matches floating in mid-air, bottles breaking for no reason, chairs flying around . . ."

Her husband persuaded people watching a brightly-lit UFO to try to communicate with it. He said: "We began uttering the letters of the alphabet, and heard sounds from behind the lights. The letter D came back long and hard. Lights started flashing everywhere, and we heard something that sounded like a beating rhythm. Then suddenly everything went dark." Lawyer Josefino de Carvalho, who watched the experiment, said: "I'm sure that we are dealing with intelligent beings." And police chief Santos said: "I now believe that on other planets in other solar systems there exist forces which can manifest themselves here."

Through Earth's windows

Aerial researchers in America think they have located two UFO windows on this world—the sleepy New England town of Winsted, Connecticut, and the Michigan Rectangle of the mid-West.

The people of Winsted have grown used to strange shapes in the sky over the last 20 years. In February 1967, a businessman was one of three witnesses who reported an object that hovered over the town for 15 minutes before disappearing with red and green flashes. Only a few nights later two girls heard lawnmower-like sounds from a barn, and saw three humanoid creatures approaching their house. A passing car frightened them off, and minutes later the girls—and their neighbour—saw a UFO rising from a nearby hill.

Later that year, a cone-shaped object with red lights was spotted on two consecutive nights, and a month later a shape flashing red and green lights was observed hovering noiselessly over trees before zooming off at high speed.

In 1968, the sightings included a very bright globe, a balloon near the Moon, and an orange moon-like shape on a night when the Moon itself could not be seen.

In 1976, 13 girl campers and their leader heard a high-pitched whine as they climbed Blueberry Mountain, just outside the town. They looked up to see a silver, flat-bottomed saucer, about 25 feet wide. It was surrounded by a purple mist and had a red dome on top. It hovered for 30 seconds before vanishing. In 1977, a policeman and three other people saw a red-topped object hovering soundlessly near the town's sewer treatment plant, and examining the ground with two yellowish-white beams of light. The same year, people saw UFOs apparently diving into the local reservoir, and splashing upwards again.

Connecticut UFO investigator Ted Thoben is one of those who believe Winsted is a window through which UFOs arrive on Earth. He says: "Windows are a magnetic deviation in the terrain, where these things slip through. But I don't believe they come from another planet. I think they exist at a different vibratory or frequency rate so that we cannot see them most of the time. They inhabit the same space that we do, and places like Winsted are the exchange point between different dimensions.

"That theory is far more logical than saying that UFOs are from outer space. For one thing, the Earth is in the boondocks of the Milky Way galaxy. I can't see that after 2,000 years, some distant planet still finds us so intriguing they could allot so much effort to come here when there are so many other planets out there."

The term Michigan Rectangle was coined by David Fideler, head of the local Anomaly Research organization. After studying reports of strange happenings from north of Kalamazoo to the Indiana state-line in the south, he said: "The rectangle may be a centre of window phenomena— in other words a gateway from the ordinary world to the supernatural, where unreality leaks into the reality of the everyday."

Fideler has chronicled strange shapes and lights in the sky as far back as 1897. There have also been many reports in the area of phantom panther-like creatures and of Bigfoot—a human-shaped creature covered in hair, with brilliant, gleaming red eyes. And Fideler says that before the white man arrived at Lake Michigan, the Indians called it Magician Lake. He believes geophysical and electromagnetic disturbances could account for the region's bizarre events.

The 1897 sightings included a brilliant white light, a huge ball of fire and a mysterious airship. A woman also reported hearing voices from the sky. In April that year, at least a dozen people watched an unexplained light fly over the center of Kalamazoo.

In 1950, a DC-4 crashed with 58 people aboard—and Fideler says a curious ball of light was seen in the sky at the time. In 1966, a policeman was among those who saw a UFO "so bright you couldn't look straight at it". Then a UFO nearly 40 feet long was spotted cruising above a highway, blinking its lights at drivers. In 1970 there was a mysterious explosion, heard four miles away, and a gaping 40-foot hole was ripped in the ice of Upper Scott Lake. Chunks of ice flew more than 100 feet from the lake.

In 1974, police cars chased a UFO for 45 minutes. It flashed white and coloured lights, moved at 35—40 mph, and kept a height of around 600 feet before vanishing. Two years later a misty, glowing figure was reported floating a few feet above the ground, and in 1978 an unusual shape shot beams of light down on to Cook nuclear power station.

Fideler says: "There are too many bewildering reports from a small area over a long period of time for them to be simply dismissed as unrelated incidents, or the ravings of crackpots."

UFOs—all in a row

The year 1954 saw an unprecedented wave of UFO sightings over central Europe—and French parapsychologist and science writer Aimé Michel found a fascinating link as he studied some of the most reliable reports. When he plotted them on a map of his country, they formed a straight line running between and beyond the towns of Bayonne and Vichy.

All they need is love

The people of a tiny town in the Arizona desert claim UFOs have been visiting them for more than 30 years. And they say they bring only one message for the human race: "We love you." The town is Childs, an isolated settlement on the East Verde River between Flagstaff and Phoenix. Clarence Hale, 64, said: "We've seen hundreds of UFOs—I first saw one 1947. We see so many of them we don't pay them any attention any more."

His wife Mamie Ruth, 62, added: "We can tell when the starships are around. We don't even have to go outside and see them any more. It's a feeling we get, a really warm and kindly feeling. It's a sort of love-thy-neighbour feeling deep inside, a feeling of humanity.

"We truly believe that aliens from outer space are trying to talk with the people of Earth. The strong feeling of love and compassion we get is their way of contacting us. They are trying to make Earth and the universe a better place to live—there is absolutely no reason to fear them."

The good neighbours claim to have provided the authorities with evidence of UFO landings—powder and strands of silvery "angel hair." Power-plant manager Cliff Johnson found five circles of the powder on his new-mown lawn one morning, each about 12 feet in diameter.

"The powder was greyish-white until I touched it," he said. "Then it turned black, like soot. There was no other evidence that anything had touched down, just those big circles of powder. Some of them had spots of ash in the middle of them."

Clarence Hale also found powder circles after watching a "starship" land outside his home. "It was about 8 A.M. and I saw it coming in over the ridge line at about 30 mph, a big saucer-shaped ship, about 200 yards long. I could see windows and portholes with lights shining through. The ship was a silver color, like metal. It landed and took off. When it left I found the powdery ash.

"I also found the angel hair. It looks like fine cobweb, but it feels synthetic. It sits on the trees and bushes after take-off. I gathered up about 30 feet of it one night, but when I wadded it up in my hand, it just vanished."

University and government laboratories which tested the powder were unable to pinpoint its chemical make-up or origin. A top research scientist for the US Geological Survey admitted: "It has got us baffled. We could not match it with anything we know on Earth."

The people of Childs believe the "angel hair" may be a device to protect humans from damage during take-offs. Kathy Soulages said: "I think it's a flame retardant. Whenever a starship comes anywhere near where it might harm someone, it ejects the material to protect us from the heat."

Terror in the outback

Eerie objects in the sky have worried the people of a small town in Australia for more than 12 years. Trucks and cars have been chased and threatened, and one man even took a shot at a UFO with his rifle.

The town is St. George, 300 miles west of Brisbane. Max Pringle, editor of the local paper which serves the 2,500 residents and the outlying farms, said: "There have been several hundred sightings since 1967, most of them by upright citizens, not the sort to look for publicity. Nobody knows why these things are scaring the wits out of the people here. God only knows what's behind it."

Pringle says he saw his first UFO in 1977. "It was orange, shaped like a football, and soaring silently about 500 feet off the ground," he recalled. "It had green flashing lights on top, and red underneath. I was stunned—I'd never seen anything like it." By 1980, he had seen at least two dozen more.

Lorry-fleet boss Jack Dyball claims he was buzzed by a

silver-grey craft in 1975 as he drove near the town in a truck. ''It headed straight for me, then suddenly pulled up and flew out of sight,'' he said. ''I tell you, it really frightened me. It wasn't a plane, it had no wings. I really thought it was going to crash into me. When it lifted off, I saw big blue flames coming out of five burners in the back.''

Rancher's son Murray Beardmore took a pot shot at an orange UFO in September 1978. It flashed red and green lights as it flew in front of a truck he and two friends were driving. Beardmore says he stopped the truck, grabbed his rifle, and fired one shot. Then, scared, they drove very fast to his home with the UFO trailing them. At one stage, their engine inexplicably cut out. The boy's father, John Beardmore, said: ''He was really shaken when he got here. All three of them were pretty ashen-faced. My sister, my wife and I all saw the thing, and got in the car to chase it, but it disappeared.''

The Broadhaven triangle

Fifty sightings in a single year

Who or what haunts the Broadhaven Triangle? It is a mystery that has baffled scientists, military investigators and UFOlogists.

The triangle lies between Swansea, mid-Wales and Broadhaven. And it has been the subject of more UFO visitations than almost anywhere else in the world. In one year alone, more than 50 positive sightings were made.

At first it was thought the rash of reports from the triangle was connected with the intense defence activity in the area. Within a tight radius there are: the Royal Aircraft Establishment Missile Range; RAF Brawdy, an operational station; The Army's Pendine Ranges; a missile testing ground; supersonic low-flying corridors, and an American submarine tracking station. Spokesmen for the establishments are nonplussed by the flood of sightings. And very few can be explained away by defence operations.

Certainly the sight that terrified Billy and Pauline Coombs

Broadhaven Primary School, showing the area beyond the school where a landed UFO was seen.

in their farm cottage has baffled the experts. They were sitting in their front room at 1 A.M. when Pauline suddenly turned to look at the window. Blocking it was a towering, eerie figure wearing a silver suit.

Too terrified to scream, Pauline stared, transfixed, at the 7-foot figure. Sensing her fear, Billy turned in his seat and saw the monstrous outline. "Good God! What the hell's that?" he yelled.

"It was wearing a helmet with some sort of shiny visor," Pauline recalled. "A pipe went from the mouth to the back of the head. I was petrified. We were rooted to the spot with terror.

"It radiated a sort of luminous light and when it touched the window, the pane started to rattle like all hell had broken loose—yet there was no wind.

"When I got my wits together, I raced upstairs to see if the children were all right. Billy put our labrador Blackie outside, but he went mad with fear. He had to be destroyed six months later."

The Coombs telephoned for help, but by the time police arrived at their home, Ripperton Farm, near the village of

Dale, Dyfed, the eerie visitor had disappeared. The couple also telephoned neighbours to report what they had seen. Billy's boss, farmer Richard Hewison, drove over as soon as he got their call. "They were genuinely terrified," he said. "They were frightened out of their wits."

The family had two souvenirs of the incident—a burned out TV set, and a rose bush near the window, which was badly scorched.

The ordeal in the early hours of April 24, 1977, was not Mrs. Coombs's first brush with the unknown. Two months earlier, on February 24, she had been driving three of her five children home from nearby St. Ishmael's shortly after 8 P.M. when one of the boys saw a light which seemed to be coming towards them at great speed.

As the children started crying with fear, Mrs. Coombs, 33 and said to be a down-to-earth type by those who knew her, put her foot on the accelerator. "I thought the thing would come through the windscreen," she recalled. "In the end it went just over us and did a tight U-turn."

The craft now flew alongside them, skimming over the tops of the hedges at 80 mph as Mrs. Coombs kept her foot down. For 10 minutes, the bizarre chase continued through deserted country lanes. The object was no bigger than a football, but glowed yellow and had a beam of light underneath.

Finally, the car came in sight of the farmhouse . . . and the engine cut out. Hysterical, Mrs. Coombs grabbed her children from the back seat and rushed into the house. As she gabbled her amazing story, her eldest son saw the object disappearing.

For a year after that, inexplicable happenings made the family's life a misery. The children frequently saw bright lights landing in the fields, and found scorch marks next morning. On a trip to the coast at nearby St. Bride's Bay, they saw two silvery-suited figures, and a flying disc which seemed to disappear into rocks. Two of the children received strange burns. Five television sets and eight cars mysteriously burned out. Then, as suddenly as the incidents had begun, they stopped.

The Coombs's neighbours also reported curious happenings. Mr. Hewison's wife Josephine looked out of the bedroom window one morning to see a 50-foot silver spacecraft standing beside her greenhouse.

She said: "It was as high as a double decker bus, there were no visible windows or openings. It stood there for about 10 minutes then took off. It left no mark. Not even a broken twig."

Teenaged shop assistant Stephen Taylor, of Haverfordwest, may have come the closest to an extra-terrestrial encounter—when a figure similar to the one that terrified the Coombs suddenly appeared by his side. He was walking home late one night when he saw a black shape in front of him.

He said: "It looked about 40 or 50 feet across. I noticed a dim glow around what seemed to be the underside. Suddenly this figure popped up, right next to me. I was terrified. It was dressed in silver. It seemed to have high cheekbones.

"Its eyes were like fish eyes—completely round. I took a swing at it and ran. I don't know whether I hit it. I ran the three miles home. When I got there, my pet dog started snarling at me. It wouldn't let me near it."

Louise Bassett, wife of a restaurant owner from Ferryside, Carmarthen, said: "I was driving home one night when my radio went dead. At the same time, I saw flashing lights in the sky. I took a detour to avoid them but they appeared again three miles further on." When Mrs. Bassett's radio cut out, so did dozens of other people's radios and televisions in the area. Mrs. Bassett's dog was in the car with her at the time. "It has never been the same since that night," she said.

Artist John Petts, 62, was working in his studio near Carmarthen when he saw a brilliant light in the sky. "It was a cigar-shaped object. One minute it was there, the next it was gone," he said.

Perhaps the best witnesses of all are the children of Broadhaven Primary School. Fifteen of them—14 boys and a girl—were playing football when they rushed inside to tell their headmaster that they had seen a spaceship in the sky.

The head, Mr. Ralph Llewellyn, split them up and asked them to draw pictures of what they had seen. He compared the finished results and was astounded by their similarity. It was no prank. Mr. Llewellyn said: "I do not believe that children of this age could sustain a hoax of this nature."

The sighting that excited investigators from the British UFO Research Association and which is regarded as the most authentic so far was by two company directors as they drove in bright daylight from Carmarthen to Newcastle Emlyn—straight through the centre of the triangle.

One of the men, Elvet Dyer, described their experience: "A huge cigar-shaped machine, at least 20 feet long, crossed our path 100 yards ahead. It was flying so low it would have taken the top off a double-decker bus. It made no sound and we thought it was going to crash.

"We braced ourselves for an explosion as it passed out of sight into a field, but when we looked into the field there was nothing there at all."

The two men, non-believers in UFOs, were badly shaken and unnerved.

Mr. Randall Pugh, regional investigator for the UFO association, said: "We know there is something very strange going on in this area. Many of the reports have been from intelligent, educated people who are not disposed to exaggerate or misconstrue what they have seen."

Dozens more reports of unexplained sights have flooded into the UFO association. Randall Pugh has noticed one common link in the sightings. "People who encounter these phenomena suffer severe headaches, trembling and sleeplessness," he said.

It is no wonder the people living in the Broadhaven Triangle are getting jittery. They believe that they have been singled out for surveillance by interplanetary beings.

A local police inspector said: "After what I've seen round here in the last few years, nothing would surprise me now."

7

Encounters of the Sinister Kind

The vast majority of UFO spotters live to
tell their tales, and are none-the-worse for
their experience. Others are not so lucky.
Several have emerged from too-close
encounters with wounds and illnesses
which defy all the medical knowledge at
our disposal. And there is other evidence
that UFOs have the frightening potential
for awesome intervention in human
affairs . . .

The beams that burn

The vast majority of UFO sightings are painless for the humans involved. Indeed, most people who claim to have seen the craft and met their occupants, stress that they mean us no harm, and are only here to help. But sometimes people do get hurt. One incident in America in 1968 gave a hint of what could happen if the UFOs ever decided to get nasty.

Gregory Wells was returning from his grandmother's home to his own house next door in Beallsville, Ohio, at about 8:30 P.M. on March 19 when he saw a large oval-shaped object hovering over nearby trees. It was red, and brilliantly lit. Suddenly a tube came out of the bottom, and moved towards the boy. A beam of light shot from it, and Gregory was knocked to the ground, screaming with fright as the upper arm of his jacket caught fire.

He was rushed to the town hospital with second-degree burns, and his scar was still visible three months later. Sheriff F. L. Suisberger of Monroe County interviewed several other people who had seen the UFO, including Gregory's mother and grandmother, and could find no other explanation for the injuries. The jacket and the road were checked for radioactivity, but none was found.

Such unprovoked attacks are mercifully rare. Others have felt the power of UFOs, but escaped unscathed. And a few have suffered agonies that were probably not intended.

A too-close encounter with a fiery diamond-shaped UFO left two American women and a child with excruciating pains that doctors were powerless to cure. Experts who questioned the victims under hypnosis were convinced they had suffered radiation burns after coming into contact with a craft manned by intelligent aliens.

Vicky Landrum, 57, and her grandson Colby, seven, were returning home to Dayton, Texas, on December 29, 1980, after attending a bingo game in Cleveland, a small town 40 miles away, with their friend Betty Cash, 52. Some 20 miles north-west of Dayton, on a desolate stretch of tree-lined road, they all noticed a glowing object lighting up the sky. "Suddenly it came down, over the trees, and into the road right in front of us," said Mrs. Landrum.

"It looked like the whole sky had split. We saw a massive blue diamond, hovering at treetop level, with huge red flames shooting down to the road. Colby started to scream, and I said, "Honey, if you see Jesus coming out of the sky, He's coming to carry us to a better place." I really thought it was the end of the world.

"Betty slammed on the brakes. She got out and started walking towards the object. It was as big as a water tank. I rolled down the window—it was getting so hot from the flames—and stuck my head out to have a good look at the thing. It was making a beep, beep sound.

"I felt my eyes starting to burn, and I called to Betty to come back, but she was standing there entranced. Colby went berserk and tried to get out and run to the woods, so I grabbed him and held him close and said, 'Don't cry, baby, just pray.'"

The diamond held them trapped for 15 minutes. Every so often, they heard a rushing sound like air brakes as bigger flames scorched down to the road. Each time the UFO lifted slightly, then settled to its previous height. Finally it rose slowly, then disappeared at high speed to the west, in the direction of Houston.

As the stunned trio continued the drive home, Mrs. Landrum told Colby: "Don't tell anybody about it—they'll think we're crazy." But it soon became clear that someone would have to be told.

Within an hour of reaching Dayton, all three were sick. Soon both Mrs. Cash and Mrs. Landrum found their skin turning beetroot-red. Their eyes began to burn and weep, and they felt that they were looking through a film or mist. By morning, Mrs. Cash found large lumps forming all over her body. She suffered agonizing headaches, and her hair was coming out in handfuls. She was so weak she could not get out of bed to call help. When the pain did not ease, she was admitted to Houston's Parkway Hospital.

During four weeks of exhaustive tests, medical experts tried to find out what was wrong with her. "The doctors and nurses kept asking if I was a burn victim," she said. "Skin was peeling off my arms and legs and face. I was blistered all over. My ears and eyes were so swollen that my own family didn't recognize me."

Mrs. Landrum also lost tufts of hair, and specialists who examined her eyes found them "burned, swollen and extremely irritated". She was warned that cataract-like films were forming which might make her blind. Her grandson suffered digestive problems, and for weeks was haunted by terrible nightmares which left him screaming every night.

Four months after their ordeal, the women were still living in a nightmare of pain and fear. "I don't know what to do," Mrs. Cash told a newspaper reporter. "I'm at my wits' end. I need help and so does Vicky. I look terrible and I'm too sick to work. There must be something that can be done to help us. We don't know where to turn."

UFO experts who investigated their case learned that the same shape had been seen 30 minutes earlier by three people driving 20 miles farther east. But none of them left their car, and none suffered ill effects.

Mrs. Landrum agreed to be hypnotized by investigators who wanted to check the authenticity of her story. During questioning, she clutched the front of her blouse, screwing the material into her fist. She was sweating profusely as she gasped: "We can't get through, it's blocking the road . . . the whole thing's burning up . . . oh my God, it's coming closer, we're going to burn up . . ."

After the sessions, Dr. Leo Sprinkle, a professor of counselling services at Wyoming University, said: "There is no doubt she had a real experience. I believe the craft was under intelligent control." NASA aerospace engineer John Schussler, who watched the sessions while investigating the case for an independent UFO organization, VISIT, said: "This is a very important case providing physical evidence of the existence of UFOs. A radiologist who examined the women's records said they were apparently suffering from the symptoms of radiation poisoning." Bill English, of the

Arizona Aerial Phenomena Research Organization, added: "It's the most incredible UFO sighting reported in the US in years."

Teenage farmworker Mark Henshall claims he was scorched by a UFO while out riding his motorbike. Mark, then 16, said he felt a prickly, heat rash sensation on his face and arms for days after the incident in June, 1976.

· He was riding the bike along a lonely country road near his home in Barnard Castle, County Durham, England, when he felt he was being watched. He looked up and saw a brilliant light in the night sky behind him, slightly to his left.

"I was riding at about 30 mph but the bike seemed to cut out," he told researchers from the UFO Investigators Network. "I was very frightened. I could feel heat on my face and through my jacket. The petrol tank was steaming. It seemed as if something was pulling my bike forwards."

A Jaguar car also spluttered to a stop nearby while Mark stood fumbling to light a cigarette. "I was trembling," he recalled. "I touched the car to steady myself and it was really hot.

"Next morning my hands and arms came out in a sort of rash which lasted for a couple of days. I've been ridiculed by my mates, but I'm sure what I saw was a flying saucer."

An American truck driver was temporarily blinded on October 3, 1973, when he stuck his head out of the vehicle's window to get a better look at a UFO in Missouri. His wife, who was with him, said a "large ball of fire" struck him in the face, knocking his glasses off. She took over the wheel and drove him to hospital, where he was treated for burns, but it was some hours before he could see again.

A physicist who examined the man's spectacles after the incident said the frames had been subjected to intense heat, and one lens had fallen out as a result.

Two people who claimed they saw a giant glowing egg, more than 35 yards long, near Baltimore, Maryland, on October 26, 1958, also needed hospital treatment later. The couple said their car stalled as they turned a corner and saw the shape hovering above a bridge. They got out and crouched behind the vehicle while they watched a brilliant light and a wave of heat flood from the UFO. Then it shot up with a thunderous roar, and was out of sight within 10 seconds. Doctors found what seemed like radiation burns on the faces of both witnesses.

Space-stunned

A drive through the snow-covered countryside of Massachusetts ended in terror beside a lonely cemetery for William Wallace and his wife. It was 1 A.M. when they arrived back at their home town, Leominster, after the 90-minute outing on March 8, 1967, and ran into a thick patch of fog by St. Leo's graveyard. Mr. Wallace drove slowly through the mist, then turned the car round and headed back into it to investigate a strange glow from the direction of the church. He feared the building might be on fire.

When he drew level with the cemetery, he parked the car and the couple stared in amazement. The glow was coming from a large object shaped like a flattened egg, several hundred feet above the ground. Despite warnings from his wife, Mr. Wallace stepped out of the car and excitedly pointed up at the object, which was ablaze with light similar to that from an acetylene torch.

As he raised his arm, the idling engine of his car cut out, and its lights and radio went dead. Mr. Wallace felt numb and immobilized. His pointing arm was dragged back by some power, and thudded against the roof of the car. "My mind was not at all affected," he said later. "I could hear my wife screaming for me to get back in the car but I just could not move. I was paralyzed for perhaps 30 or 40 seconds. Then the object, which had been rocking back and forwards, began to move slowly away before shooting up and out of the fog. Abruptly the car lights and radio came back on, and I could move again, slowly and sluggishly."

The couple drove home carefully, then phoned their parents and the police. Local officers knew them as reliable people, not liable to scare easily. But they were really shaken as they told of their eerie encounter.

Temporary paralysis of witnesses has been noted in several other UFO sightings.

On June 14, 1964, 18-year-old Charles Englebrecht was watching TV alone at home in Dale, Indiana, when a bright light flashed past his window, and the electricity failed. Groping his way to the door of the house, he saw a brilliantly lit round object hovering 50 feet from him. But as he started to walk towards it, a tingling sensation swept over his body, and he found he could not move. The sensation ended when the object disappeared, leaving behind a strong smell of sulfur and burned rubber. Local police who investigated also smelt the sulfur, and found a scorched area of earth, the size of a large dinner plate, plus three shallow indentations which could have been left by tripod legs.

A day later, William Angelos was also watching TV late at night in Lynn, Massachusetts, when a loud roaring sound interrupted him. He rushed outside his apartment block and saw a domed object with an inverted, red glowing cone underneath, slowly rising from the car-parking area. As he moved towards it, he too felt a tingling sensation sweep up his body from his feet, until he was immobilized. Only when the object was out of sight did movement return to his muscles.

Bolt from the blue

Did a laser beam from a UFO destroy two houses in Kuala Lumpur, Malaysia, in 1980? Police investigating the blazes which gutted the homes were told by three witnesses that a red ball of light had hovered above the buildings in the Port Klang district before the fire. Suddenly, from about 100 feet up, a bolt of blue light shot towards the earth, and the houses burst into flames.

Neither man accepted suggestions that fear had frozen his limbs; and Mr. Wallace swore that, when his arm was pinned to the roof of his car, it felt as though some power was pulling it backwards. Could it be that UFOs have directional forces similar to the stun guns of science fiction stories? The effects were all temporary, indicating that the UFO intelligence has a good understanding of human limitations and endurance.

The air crash death of Captain Thomas Mandtell, described earlier, shows that UFOs may have the power to kill if seriously threatened. But there have also been UFO-related deaths for which no immediate motive was apparent . . .

Death by appointment

It was the strangest case Inspector José Bittencourt of the Rio de Janeiro homicide squad had ever faced. In August, 1966, two small boys found the bodies of Manuel Cruz and Miguel Viana lying on the top of Vintem Hill, a 1,000-foot-high vantage point overlooking the small town of Niteroi. Beside them were: crudely-made lead masks, only inches from their faces; pieces of green and blue paper, one of which contained a formula that no one could decipher, and two notes, neither of which made much sense.

The first note read: "Sunday, one pill after meal. Monday, one pill after breakfast. Tuesday, one pill after meal. Wednesday, one pill lying down."

The other said: "4:30 P.M. be at appointed place. 6:30 swallow pill. Then protect face with metal and wait for signal to show itself."

The two men were both wearing raincoats over their ordinary clothes. A post-mortem examination revealed that they had died within seconds of each other. Two doctors reported: "All organs had been functioning normally. After detailed investigation, it is impossible to find the cause of death."

Bittencourt at first thought the men had been murdered

for money they were carrying. He checked at their home town of Campos, and found that they had taken a bus for Rio with £1,000 of cruzeiros in their pockets, ostensibly to buy a car. When their bodies were found, there was only money worth £30 left, and the men had gone nowhere near a car showroom.

Instead they had left the bus at Niteroi, bought two raincoats from shopkeeper Jaime Alves—even though the day was scorching hot—and set off up Vintem Hill.

Bittencourt then put two statements together, and came up with an astonishing alternative theory. On the night that the two Brazilian television engineers had climbed the hill, stockbroker's wife Gracinda Souza reported seeing a green and yellow circular object, reddish at the rim, flash across the sky and glide towards the summit.

And in Campos, Miguel's father and a friend revealed that the two men had been obsessed with space communications, and had conducted experiments, one of which had resulted in an explosion and strange lights. "I think they somehow contacted a flying saucer," said Miguel's father. "They were killed because they knew too much."

Anywhere else in the world, police would have dismissed such a theory as nonsense. But Bittencourt was familiar with UFOs. He worked in the 100,000 square miles of Brazil known, because of frequent sightings, as Flying Saucer Alley.

No alternative explanation for the deaths was ever found, and eventually the file closed. Police were convinced that the men were not killed where they were found. Had they really been taken aboard a spacecraft, their bodies returned by the disc seen by Mrs. Souza? Were they indeed killed because they had discovered a secret, because of their knowledge?

The mystery had one more baffling twist to it. The strange formula found beside the bodies was locked in a police vault. But when the safe was next opened, the paper had vanished.

On the other side of the world, the town of Martinsicuro, near Pescara, in southern Italy, was plunged into mourning when, on October 12, 1978, brothers Gianfranco and Vittorio De Fulgentiis were found dead in the Mediterranean.

But police trying to find out how they died were baffled. Their fishing boat was found undamaged on the sea-bed. And nobody could explain the peculiar puncture marks on the two men's faces.

Then other fishermen reported seeing red balls of light in the sky, following their boats. And Lieutenant-Colonel Piero Gallerano, of the Pescara police department, began to think again about earlier stories he had dismissed.

"I had received reports before from sailors about strange lights in the sky, and did not believe a word," he said. "Now I learn that these lights often follow boats.

"A navy patrol boat saw a red light at sea level. This light shot up about 300 meters and disappeared. The boat's radar and radio jammed. The red disc was gone in about four seconds. We are sure it was not a signal rocket. It was a very fast unidentifiable flying object."

Suddenly, UFOs were no longer a laughing matter in Martinsicuro.

Animals at risk

Did a flying saucer kill 15 ponies on Dartmoor? Members of the Devon Unidentified Flying Objects Centre believe it did. The dead ponies were found close together in a little valley miles from any of the roads over the moors. Their bones were crushed, their ribs were cracked, and their flesh had rotted away to leave bare skeletons in only 48 hours, far quicker than normal.

Four UFO investigators took over the case in July 1975 after animal experts declared themselves baffled. They searched the area with geiger counters and metal detectors; and though they found nothing, the group leader John Wyse, a bandsman in the army, said: "I think the ponies were crushed by the anti-gravity field of a flying saucer as it took off."

A UFO was also the prime suspect when animals died mysteriously in a zoo at Newquay, Cornwall. Three ducks, a goose, a swan and two baby wallabies were found dead on the morning after strange lights were reported over the town. One bird was decapitated. Detectives were said to have discovered that the bodies gave off positive radiation readings.

In Minnesota, top American UFO investigator Dr. J. Allen Hynek was called in after farm animals were found mutilated. There were no human footprints near the bodies, and no signs of attack by predators. Internal organs appeared to have been removed by surgical instruments, and many cows had had their blood sucked out.

Dr. Hynek said that 22 cattle were killed during the late 1960s and that curious deaths recurred in 1973 around the towns of Canby, Viking, Warroad and Kimball. He appealed for farmers to contact him at his UFO Centre in Evanston, Illinois, whenever they found more bodies.

Apart from making life painful for humans—and possibly holding the power of life and death over both man and animals—UFOs may have the ability to control some of Earth's most sophisticated scientific achievements . . .

Unexplained power failures

Can UFOs black out cities?

The plant manager at Consolidated Edison was satisfied that all was in order as darkness fell on New York City on November 9, 1965. The system had plenty of power in reserve to meet the peak demand at dusk. But minutes after the city lights went on, they dimmed briefly, for no reason. A quick equipment check showed everything working normally, but monitoring machines registered an immense and unusual flow of current to the north. A phone call to the next station up the line, near Syracuse, confirmed that something odd had happened even farther north. Then, at 5:27 P.M., the entire city of New York was blacked out.

As the power chaos spread, the whole of the eastern seaboard of northern America and southern Canada fell into darkness. Next morning, President Johnson ordered an immediate Federal investigation. Consolidated Edison blamed transmission lines north of Niagara Falls. But the Canadian government's Electric Power Commission said a high voltage line south of the Falls was responsible. They said Ontario's Queenstown relay station had been hit by "a surge of electricity . . . flowing in the opposite direction to the normal flow at that hour." Much of Toronto and the surrounding area had had to be blacked out at 5:15 to prevent damage to expensive equipment.

Later a joint US-Canadian statement admitted that the investigators "still don't know the origin of the source of power that ripped out the relay." And in April 1966, Oscar Bakke, eastern regional director of the US Federal Power Commission's Bureau of Power told Congress that electrical workers insisted that the blackout should not—even could not—have happened.

So why did 36 million people lose power over an area of 8,000 square miles? If there was nothing wrong with generating equipment, some outside agency must have interfered with the supplies. The Aerial Phenomena Research Organization sent investigators from its base at Tucson, Arizona. And their findings were startling.

At 5:14 P.M., just 60 seconds before the Canadian blackouts, pilot Weldon Ross was flying a passenger towards Hancock Field. As they passed over the two 345,000-volt power lines carrying supplies from Niagara to the Mohawk Power Corporation's sub-station at Clay, just outside Syracuse, NY, Ross was astonished to see what he described as a bright red fireball, about 100 feet in diameter, rising from the power lines.

Ten minutes later, at the blacked-out Hancock Field airstrip, deputy aviation commissioner Robert Walsh was arranging emergency lighting for the incoming plane when he spotted a similar fireball a few miles to the south—also hovering over the power lines. New York was in darkness two minutes later.

Could UFOs have caused the most famous blackout in history? Dr. James E. McDonald, senior scientist at the Institute for Atmospheric Physics at the University of Arizona, certainly thought they could. On July 29, 1968, he gave evidence to a UFO symposium requested by the Committee on Science and Astronautics of the US House of Representatives.

After saying that UFOs had caused the fillings in people's teeth to hurt, and had been responsible for the failure of ten cars' ignition systems at Levelland, Texas, in 1957, he astounded the politicians by declaring: "UFOs have often been seen hovering near power facilities, and there are a small number—too many to seem pure, fortuitous chance— of system outrages coincident with a UFO sighting.

"After the New York blackout, I interviewed a woman in Seacliff, NY. She saw a disc hovering and going up and down, then shooting away from New York just after the power failure. I went to the Federal Power Commission for data. They didn't take them seriously, although they had many dozens of sighting reports for that famous evening. There were reports all over New England in the midst of that blackout and five witnesses near Syracuse saw a glowing object ascending within about a minute of the blackout.

"It is rather puzzling that the pulse of current that tripped the relay at Ontario has never been identified . . . there is a series of puzzling and slightly disturbing coincidences here which I think warrant much more attention than they have so far received."

If the authorities were reluctant to probe the coincidences, UFO enthusiasts were not. The National Investigations Committee on Aerial Phenomena files showed that UFOs had been sighted over Mogi Mirim, Brazil, and Tamaroa, Illinois, during 1957 power failures. Rome was in darkness in August, 1958, when a luminous flying object was spotted over the Italian capital, and a similar coincidence was reported 11 months later from Salta, Argentina.

News agency reports from Umberlandia, Minais Gerais, Brazil, on August 17, 1959, told of automatic keys at a power station being turned off as a round UFO flew along the transmission lines, then being switched on again, restoring normal service, when the UFO vanished.

Observers also noted a series of curious blackouts in late 1965 and 1966, a time when worldwide UFO activity was at fever pitch. San Salvador was without power for an hour for undisclosed reasons on November 9. Toledo, Ohio, mysteriously blacked out two days later. Relays tripped at Lima, Peru (November 19), Texas and New Mexico (December 2) and Buenos Aires, Argentina (December 26). High consumption was blamed when parts of London plunged into darkness on November 15, and in East Texas the lights inexplicably went out on December 4—just as Federal Power Commission chairman Joseph C. Swidler was explaining his New England investigations to President Johnson at the Texas White House.

At Cuernavaca, Mexico, the governor, mayor and a military zone chief all saw a glowing disc hovering at low altitude when power mysteriously cut out. And at St. Paul, Minnesota, power officials, police and residents all spotted UFOs on November 26 when sudden, unexplained electricity losses hit the city. Car lights and radios also failed as the UFO, described as huge, bright blue and glowing "like someone welding in the sky" crossed the area.

All of southern Italy lost power for up to two hours on January 8, 1966, and no reason was ever announced. Five days later, when 75 square miles of Franklin County, Maine, were blacked out, the local electricity company blamed "an apparent equipment failure which somehow corrected itself."

The spate of mysterious failures, coinciding with such concentrated UFO activity, convinced UFO believers that aliens were showing a growing interest in Earth's electricity production. But even they had no answer to the next question: were they interfering with it intentionally or inadvertently? And if the meddling was deliberate, what other powers do the UFOs have?

American defence chiefs fear their electro-magnetic power could play havoc with the sophisticated electrical systems controlling nuclear warheads. Pentagon experts were worried after several unidentified craft were spotted over their Minuteman Intercontinental Ballistic Missile sites in 1966 and 1967, and over sensitive nuclear silos and bomber bases in Maine, Michigan and Montana in 1975.

One incident caused special concern. On August 25,

1966, radio transmissions were interrupted in a concrete bunker 60 feet below the surface of a North Dakota missile base at the same time as UFOs were observed 100,000 feet above. Those interviewed about the incident were sworn to secrecy. And in 1975, a directive from the Air Force Secretary instructed public relations personnel to avoid linking sightings over nuclear bases unless specifically asked.

Skyway robbery

Mystery of the vanished satellites

Have UFOs snatched satellites sent up from Earth, so that they can study our space knowledge? Robert Barry thinks they have. Barry, head of Twentieth Century UFO Bureau in Yoe, Pennsylvania, put his theory forward after experts announced they were baffled by the disappearance of the $20 million communications satellite Satcom 3.

The one-ton orbiting unit, designed to relay telephone and television transmissions, simply vanished while working perfectly. Jim Kukowski, one of the NASA staff who helped launch it, said: "We just don't know what happened to it."

And John Williamson, a spokesman for RCA, which owned the satellite, admitted: "We've lost it and we have no idea why."

He added: "If the satellite had exploded, at least one part would have shown up on radar. The North American Air Defense Command can track an object no bigger than a basketball 23,000 miles up, so they would have certainly located something.

"If the satellite had been pushed into a different orbit by a malfunction of the engine, NORAD would again have located it when it reached its nearest point to Earth. That hasn't happened either."

Robert Barry believes aliens grabbed the satellite to examine it for information. He said: "I suppose they'd want the same thing from it as we would want from one of their spaceships.

The Scottish saucers

The British UFO Research Association launched a major investigation in the Scottish border regions in May 1981 after two women reported a series of strange sightings.

Mrs. Mary Watson and Mrs. Joyce Byers, both of Moffat, Dumfries, said they had logged more than 100 separate UFO sightings in a diary provided by Eskdalemuir Observatory. "We have noted everything from swirling, saucer-shaped objects to orange and red triangles," said Mrs. Byers.

The women said they believed the Moffat Hills might be a base for UFOs, and that there could be a link with a series of mysterious plane crashes in the border country, in which 12 people had died. They also pointed out that two nuclear power stations, Chapelcross and Windscale, were within easy flying distance.

Stuart Campbell of the UFO Research Association said: "Inquiries are being made. The two women are not the sort to make up stories."

"Someone out there is showing a lot of interest in our activities down here. UFOs are usually reported in heavy concentrations around Cape Canaveral before a launch.

"This isn't the first time a satellite has vanished mysteriously. The Soviet Molniya satellite disappeared the same way, and we know our Gemini missions and the Soviets' Salyut space lab were buzzed by UFOs."

Barry added: "Just imagine if they had plucked a manned spacecraft from orbit. The implications would be tremendous."

8

Encounters of the Aerial Kind

Mankind has always been suspicious of anything he cannot understand or control—and UFOs have been no exception. For centuries we could only watch the skies and wonder. Now we too have the means of flight. From planes and spacecraft, we can observe other flying objects at closer quarters. We can even try to attack them . . . at our peril.

Air mysteries

Dead pilots and vanished planes

The best planes and pilots Earth can muster have taken off to challenge UFOs in the sky—and all have been found wanting. In the late 1940s and early 1950s, when US Air Force aces were under orders to shoot down aerial intruders, not one victim was claimed. But the interceptors suffered casualties.

On January 7, 1948, USAF Captain Thomas Mantell led three F51 Mustang fighters into action after Kentucky police were inundated with reports of a hovering "giant air machine," in the form of a glowing disc 300 feet across. The control tower staff at Godman Field air base had seen it as well.

Mantell was an experienced pilot, a veteran of World War Two air battles. He closed in on the silvery shape over Fort Knox. "It's a disc," he radioed to Godman. "It looks metallic and is tremendous in size . . . it has a ring and a dome, and I can see rows of windows . . . the thing is gigantic, it's flying unbelievably fast. It's going up . . . I'll climb to 20,000 feet . . ."

Then the voice cut out and the radio went dead. Two hours later the wreckage of the plane was found scattered over an area a mile wide. Mantell's body lay nearby. The authorities refused to let anybody see it.

Top-level inquiries were held; but the findings, announced 18 months later, were unbelievable. The Air Force announced that Captain Mantell had probably fainted from lack of oxygen as he climbed to 20,000 feet—and what he had seen was probably the planet Venus. A planet with windows? A planet chased by an experienced pilot? Later statements changed the story. The object was simply a naval research balloon.

In June 1953, an F-94C jet fighter-interceptor took off

from Otis Air Force base on Cape Cod after a UFO had been reported. At 1,500 feet the engine cut out and the entire electrical system failed. As the aircraft's nose dipped towards the ground, pilot Captain Suggs yelled at his radar officer, Lieutenant Robert Barkoff, to bale out.

Normal procedure was for the radar officer to pull a lever which triggered explosive bolts to jettison the canopy. He then pulled a second lever, which ejected him and his seat from the plane, and when the pilot heard the second explosion, he pulled his own ejection lever. Captain Suggs baled out before he heard the second explosion, because the jet was already down to 600 feet and only seconds away from crashing.

Suggs landed just after his parachute opened in the back yard of a house. The owner, sitting near an open window, was astonished. Suggs was equally amazed. Why had the man not heard the plane crash? And where was the radar officer?

A full-scale search was launched. Cape Cod was combed on foot and from the air, and divers scoured nearby Buzzard's Bay. When the hunt was called off three months later, not a trace of the jet or of Lieutenant Barkoff had been found. They had seemingly disappeared.

On November 23, 1953, Lieutenant Felix Moncla and radar officer Lieutenant R. R. Wilson took off from Kinross Air Force Base to chase a UFO spotted over Lake Superior by Air Defense Command radar operators. The F-89C jet was guided towards the object from the ground, and controllers saw the plane close in on the UFO blip. Then, 160 miles from the base, at 8,000 feet and 73 miles off Keeweenaw Point, Michigan, the two blips merged and faded from the screen. The jet and its occupants were never seen again.

At first the Air Force said the F-89C had identified the UFO as a C47 of the Royal Canadian Air Force. But the RCAF denied that any of its planes was in the area. The official line was "that the pilot probably suffered from vertigo and crashed into the lake."

Pilot and co-pilot both survived the next disastrous attempt to intercept a UFO, but four civilians were not so lucky. On July 2, 1954, an F-94C was diverted from a routine training flight by Rome Air Force base after reports of a balloon-like object over the village of Walesville, New York. Radar scanners had shown two unidentified tracks. The first turned out to be a Canadian C47, but the second could not be identified.

What happened next was contained in an official report of the incident by Air Force investigators. "As the pilot started a descent," it said, "he noted that the cockpit temperature increased abruptly. The increase in temperature caused the pilot to scan the instruments. The fire warning light was on . . . the engine was shut down and both crew members ejected successfully."

The plane crashed in Walesville, hitting two buildings and a car. Four people were killed, two of them children. The Air Force dismissed the second object seen by radar operators as "probably a balloon."

Why did the Air Force cover up what really happened in all four incidents? Documents released since 1954 reveal that, contrary to statements at the time, there was a genuine belief that the objects chased by the jet were craft manned by intelligent beings.

As early as September 23, 1947, Lieutenant General

Double saucer over the Thames

The British Air Ministry was forced to take an interest in UFOs in 1955 when Flight Lieutenant James Salandin filed a report of a strange encounter over the Thames Estuary. He was flying his Meteor jet fighter at 16,000 feet in a cloudless sky when he spotted a metallic silver object approaching him. He described it as two saucers joined together, with a dome or bubble on top. He saw no visible portholes or jet pipes, and estimated that the craft, about 40 feet wide, was traveling at twice his 600 mph.

A Venusian spacecraft photographed in the summer of 1956.

A UFO from the constellation of Coma Berenices containing nine people who talked with the photographer for 90 minutes.

A spinning UFO seen at Joshua Tree, California, USA.

A UFO seen near Holloman Air Development Centre, New Mexico, on October 16, 1957.

A close-up of a UFO over Barra da Tijuca, Brazil, May 7, 1952.

N. F. Twining of Air Materiel Command had sent a memorandum to Brigadier-General George Schulgen, Commanding General of the Army Air Forces, saying: "It is the opinion (of this Command) that the so-called flying discs phenomenon is something real and not visionary or fictitious . . . The reported operating characteristics, such as extreme rates of climb, manoeuverability and evasive action when sighted or contacted by friendly aircraft and radar lend belief to the possibility that some of the objects are controlled either manually, automatically or remotely."

The immediate suspicion of the Americans was that the discs might be some spectacular advanced technology that the Russians had captured from the Nazis during World War Two. After the Mantell crash, an urgent investigation of possible threats to national security was launched. In August 1948, the Air Technical Intelligence Centre drew up a top-secret report concluding that UFOs were not of Russian origin, but were interplanetary craft. Air Force Chief of Staff General Hoyt S. Vandenburg ordered: "Burn it." And on December 27, 1948, the ATIC study on UFOs, code-named Project Sign, was wound up. The public were told: "Reports of flying saucers are the result of misinterpretation of various conventional objects, a mild form of mass hysteria, and hoaxes. Continuance of the project is unwarranted."

But the project was not closed down. In February 1949, it resumed inquiries under a new code-name—Project Grudge. UFO sightings continued, and in 1952 a new upsurge of reports forced the government to act again.

On July 26 of that year, three F-94 jet fighters scrambled to investigate a cluster of curious lights which appeared above the White House in Washington. The lights had also been spotted a week earlier, but this time there were more of them, nearly a dozen, zigzagging erratically at high speed.

Two of the intercepting pilots found no trace of them. But the third said he flew straight into a group of the whitish-blue lights, which travelled alongside him for 15 seconds before dispersing. All three planes returned safely, and the lights—labeled the "Washington Invasion" by the Press—were never seen again.

That month, the UFO investigating team—now working under the diplomatically more acceptable title of Project Bluebook—were receiving between 20 and 30 sightings every day, 20 per cent of them objects that no one could identify or explain away. Embarrassingly for touchy Air Force chiefs, one of the witnesses was Dan Kimball, the Secretary of State for the American Navy. He said two disc-shaped UFOs buzzed the plane in which he was flying to Hawaii, circling it twice before shooting off at more than 1,500 mph, then repeating the exercise round a Navy plane 50 miles away.

When Kimball later inquired what progress Bluebook was making on his report, he was told that no action had been taken and that officers were forbidden to discuss case analysis with anyone. Furthermore, no copies of reports could be returned.

Scientists who knew too much?

Suicide verdicts were recorded on two top US scientists who died after studying UFOs, having decided that they were extraterrestrial spaceships investigating life on Earth. Atmospheric physician Professor James McDonald, of the University of Arizona, was found with a bullet in his head in 1971, and astronomer Professor Robert Jessup was discovered in his gas-filled car in 1959. A friend of Jessup claimed: "He knew too much, they wanted him out of the way." But fellow scientists felt both men had suffered depression after battling for years against a brick wall of governmental UFO denials and evasions, and the scorn of skeptical colleagues.

By 1953, public pressure for information about UFOs forced the Central Intelligence Agency (CIA) to make some sort of gesture. It convened the Robertson Panel, under a respected Californian scientist, H. P. Robertson, and asked it to evaluate UFOs. There were three possible findings, that UFOs were explainable objects and natural phenomena, that there was insufficient data in reports to make a conclusion, or that UFOs were interplanetary spacecraft.

According to Edward Ruppelt, former chief of the Air Force UFO Project, the panel opted for the second possibility, and urged that Bluebook manpower be quadrupled, bringing in skilled scientists and observers to try to solve the problem of what UFOs really were. It also recommended that the public be told "every detail of every phase" of UFO investigations. Privately, said Ruppelt, almost every member of the panel was convinced that UFOs were extraterrestrial.

The CIA suppressed the report, finally releasing a censored version of it in 1966. And they ignored its recommendations, instigating instead a "debunking" programme. A secret document released years later read: "The debunking aim would result in reduction of public interest in flying saucers which today evokes a strong psychological reaction. This education could be accomplished by mass media such as television, motion pictures and popular articles. Basis of such education would be actual case histories which had been puzzling at first but later explained. As in the case of conjuring tricks, there is much less stimulation if the secret is known."

While the public was told that UFOs did not exist, servicemen were ordered to shoot them down. People who reported seeing flying saucers were ridiculed. Forces personnel were threatened with jail or fines if they broadcast what they had seen. "Only false statements and fictitious reports may be published," read one Air Force order. "All real reports must be treated as secret and forwarded to the appropriate authorities."

Once the Americans realized that UFOs were not a Soviet secret weapon, the race was on to capture one before the Russians did. Insight into such advanced technology would be of incalculable value to either power. Meanwhile, public debunking of UFOs might make the Russians less interested in trying to bring one down.

The ploy did not work. Moscow had come to the same conclusions as Washington. In 1957, anti-aircraft batteries around the Soviet capital opened up on an object in the sky—until the guns' electrical systems mysteriously went dead.

In 1967, American Air Force agents monitored a broadcast from one of two Cuban jet fighters sent up to intercept a curious UFO. The pilot said he had just seen his partner's plane disintegrate without smoke or flames as he tried to shoot the object down. Stanton Friedman, who revealed the story after leaving his job as a space-related nuclear technician for the US government, claimed that tapes of the conversation were sent to the National Security Agency, which ordered the loss to be listed as equipment malfunction.

Not all UFOs proved so lethal. One spotted above the English counties of Norfolk, Suffolk, and Cambridgeshire in 1956 seemed almost playful when a plane came close. The excitement started at 9:30 P.M. on August 13 when radar operators at U.S.A.F. Bentwaters spotted an object which zoomed off the screen at what seemed to be 5,000 mph. Then a group of slow-moving shapes were tracked out to sea. They seemed to link up into one object before disappearing with a stop-go-stop motion. More sightings were reported at 10 P.M. and again at 10:55 P.M. when observers saw a blurred white light pass overhead. A C-47 aircraft radioed that it had passed below them at extraordinary speed.

Bentwaters alerted radar crews farther north at Lakenheath, and they too saw the object, on screen and visually. Its antics were baffling, changing direction crazily, shooting off at right angles without stopping, and scorching to enormous speeds from a standing start.

Two jet fighters diverted to intercept could find no trace of the object. Then a Venom single-seat fighter, equipped with nose radar, took off from Waterbeach, and was guided from the ground towards the UFO, at that stage motionless

The foo fighters of World War Two

A secret new German weapon was revealed to the world on December 13, 1944. An Associated Press report filed from Paris said "mysterious silvery balls which float in the air" had been seen on the Western Front, and added: "It is possible that they represent a new anti-aircraft defence instrument."

Only after the war was it revealed that the balls were not sent up by the Germans. Their forces had seen them too—and thought they were a British or American device. Pilots from either side in both Europe and the Pacific war zone had seen similar shapes flying alongside them on bombing raids, sometimes in formation. The Allies had christened them "foo fighters," a work derived from a popular comic-strip catchphrase, "Where there's foo, there's fire." The official verdict was that the balls were electrical phenomena called St. Elmo's fire, but many of the pilots thought they knew better.

and clearly visible, between 15,000 and 29,000 feet, over Lakenheath.

The pilot radioed that he had radar contact and "gun-lock"—then he lost sight of his quarry. "Where did he go?" he asked ground control. "Roger, it appears he got behind you and he's still there," came the reply. The UFO had zipped into position in an incredible right-angled flight too fast for most of the radar watchers to follow. Once behind the Venom, it had split into two separate units, one behind the other, and locked on to the fighter.

A bizarre game of hide and seek began. For ten minutes, the Venom pilot dived, climbed and circled, trying to shake off his pursuer. But the UFO stuck to his tail, always 100–200 yards behind. Finally the Venom headed for home, its fuel running low. The UFO followed it down, then stopped, hovered in triumph for a while, and vanished.

Cynics pointed out that the East Anglian terrain is notorious for generating false radar traces, known as "angels," and that the incident occurred at the climax of the Perseid meteor shower, which passes Earth each year and appears as a series of luminous white blobs.

But the official report on the incident, filed on August 31 by Captain Edward Holt of the 81st Fighter-Bomber Wing, Bentwaters, said: "The object . . . followed all manoeuvers of the jet fighter aircraft."

Nearly a year later, the six-man crew of a US Air Force RB-47 jet reported another playful UFO. It chased them for more than 1½ hours in a 1,000-mile flight across Mississippi, Louisiana, Texas and Oklahoma early on the morning of June 17, 1957. Curiously, they added, the object occasionally vanished from sight momentarily—and when it did so, it also disappeared from their radar screen, only to reappear within seconds in the same place.

The debunking of UFOs worked quite well for a while. Project Bluebook successfully managed to "investigate" sightings, and to produce unsatisfactory answers. Then, in 1964 and again in 1967, came fresh waves of UFO activity. In response to renewed public pressure, the Air Force announced that renowned physicist Dr. Edward Condon would lead a University of Colorado inquiry into the sightings, to run parallel with the Bluebook investigations.

In January 1969, Condon's report said: "Careful consideration of the record as it is available to us leads us to conclude that further extensive study of the UFOs probably cannot be justified in the expectation that science will be advanced thereby." It admitted, however, that 30 percent of cases it investigated remained unexplained.

The 1,000-page report was condemned as a whitewash—and worse. One UFO research group pulled out of the investigations because of Condon's negative and subjective comments; and two of the inquiry team, Dr. Norman LeVine and Dr. David Saunders, were fired for leaking a memorandum that read: "The trick would be, I think, to describe the project so that, to the public, it would appear a totally objective study but, to the scientific community, would present the image of a group of non-believers trying their best to be objective but having an almost zero expectation of finding a saucer."

The memo was written by assistant project director Dr. Robert Low, whose job was to coordinate the inquiry. The two doctors were not alone in having no confidence in him. Condon's administrative assistant quit, saying: "Bob's attitude from the beginning has been one of negativism."

Criticism of the Condon Report was loud and long. Congressman J. Edward Roush told the House of Representatives that he had "grave doubts as to the scientific profundity and objectivity of the project." He added: "We are $500,000 poorer and not richer in information about UFOs . . . I am not satisfied and the American public will not be satisfied." Aviation pioneer John Northrop, the 80-year-old founder of Northrop Aircraft Company and co-founder of Lockheed, said: "The 21st century will die laughing at the Condon Report."

The Condon inquiry did one service for the subject of UFOs. The fact that such a distinguished scientist was prepared to study them allowed other top boffins to take UFOs seriously as well. Even after he debunked them, others felt free to continue their studies without fear of ridicule. And though the Air Force announced, on December 17, 1969, that it was closing down Project Bluebook because UFOs "didn't exist," it too continued to monitor and analyze reports through the Aerospace Defence Command.

In the 1970s, laws concerning freedom of information, and the more enlightened attitudes of other governments, notably France and Italy, and even Russia, allowed greater access to UFO reports, and there were more frequent reports of confrontations between unidentified objects and Earth aircraft.

A squadron of F-106 jet fighters scrambled in 1975 when a fleet of mysterious shapes appeared at 15,000 feet over Montana. As they approached the shining lights, the objects simply vanished.

An even stranger encounter emerged only a few years after it happened. Captain Lawrence Coyne and three crewmen took off in a US Air Force helicopter from Columbus, Ohio, at 10:30 P.M. on October 18, 1973, heading for Cleveland. Forty minutes later, they were 2,500 feet up over Mansfield when one of the men noticed a red light approaching from the east at high speed. Coyne dived to 1,700 feet but a collision seemed inevitable. He braced himself for the impact. It never came.

About 500 feet away from the helicopter, the UFO stopped abruptly. Coyne noticed a huge grey metallic hull, about 60 feet long and shaped like a streamlined fat cigar. The front edge glowed red, green lights flickered at the back, and there was a dome in the centre. A green light suddenly swivelled and flooded the helicopter cockpit. Coyne tried to radio an SOS, but his set would not transmit or receive. Then he looked at his instrument panel and gasped. The helicopter was being lifted into the air.

"I could hardly believe it," he said. "The altimeter was reading 3,500 feet, climbing to 3,800. I had made no attempt to pull up. All the controls were still set for a 20-degree dive. Yet we had climbed from 1,700 feet to 3,500 with no power in a couple of seconds, with no G-forces or other noticeable strains. There was no noise or turbulence either."

Finally the crew felt a slight bounce, and the UFO zipped

away towards the north-west. Seven minutes later, the helicopter radio started working normally again, and Coyne reported the incident to incredulous ground controllers.

Phantoms versus UFOs

One early morning in September 1976, an F-4 Phantom jet fighter streaked into the skies of Iran from Shahrokhi Air Force base. It had been ordered to investigate a dazzling bright light spotted by hundreds of people south of Tehran. The fighter closed on the object, but when it was 30 miles away, all radio contact was lost.

As the pilot broke off and headed back to Shahrokhi, his radio crackled back to life, and he reported that all communications and instrumentation systems in the plane had suddenly and inexplicably cut out.

A second Phantom was already in the air and in pursuit of the UFO at a speed much greater than the speed of sound; but the craft was still accelerating away from it. The pilot, Lieutenant Fafari, radioed that it seemed about the size of a 707 passenger aircraft. Suddenly the UFO released a smaller, disc-shaped object which also glowed brilliantly. It hurtled straight for the jet.

Fafari reached for his weapon control panel and pressed a button to release an AIM-9 air-to-air missile. Nothing happened. All his electrical systems had blacked out. He swung his defenceless plane into a dive to avoid the approaching disc, which changed course to follow him for four miles. Then it zoomed back to the larger UFO.

As Fafari's instruments started working again, he again went after the ''mother ship,'' which was moving away rapidly. Then it shed another disc, which fell at great speed towards the Earth. Fafari watched it go down, expecting an explosion, but it stopped just above some hills, casting an eerie glow over a two-mile area. Fafari looked up again, and realized that the larger UFO had used the disc to distract him while it vanished. He returned safely to base. The

Iranian government later filed reports of the incident to the Pentagon in Washington. A year later the Italian government revealed that its jets had also encountered UFOs. It listed six separate encounters during 1977 and 1978, two of which involved air force personnel, and one a civilian airliner. On February 23, 1977, a fighter pilot spotted an intense ball of light over Milan. "When radar gave me authorization to intercept, the object went up to 12,000 feet and kept its distance," he said. "It was in my sight for 23 minutes."

On October 27 of the same year, a football-shaped UFO buzzed a helicopter during NATO exercises at Elmas Air Force base, near Cagliari, Sardinia. The Defence Ministry quoted an air controller as saying: "I saw a UFO that flew at the speed of a jet, around 565 mph. It was behind a helicopter that was participating in military maneuvers." Three other helicopter pilots and jet fighter crews also reported seeing the UFO, which flew alongside some of them. Later a jet was sent up to intercept a separate cigar-shaped object, but it proved too fast.

Three other sightings in the Italian report were by air traffic controllers using binoculars. At Naples on August 4, 1977, officials watched a pulsating star-shaped object for 90 minutes. At Elmas on November 5, a UFO was observed for eight minutes, during which it rose from 5,000 feet to 30,000 in 30 seconds. And at Pisa on November 23, staff saw a strange glowing shape change colour from red to violet to green for two hours at 15,000 feet.

The last of the objects, all listed as "genuine UFOs," was seen on March 9, 1978. The pilot of International Airlines flight IH-662 radioed Milan control tower to report "a green rocket moving above and below us about a mile away." He asked if it could be another aircraft, and was told none were in the area.

"I thought I was going mad," the pilot later told officials who interviewed him. "I only reported the sighting for information. When other pilots said they had seen it too, I knew I wasn't seeing things."

Three Austrian air force jets took to the sky on May 7, 1980, after a KLM liner pilot told Vienna air controllers that a grey spherical object was flying above him over the Dachstein mountains. Two of the fighters were ordered to intercept, while the third filmed the confrontation. But both missions proved impossible. All three made visual contact with the object, but could not get close because of its unpredictable, erratic behavior. It soon vanished completely.

Action over the Arctic

Russian pilots have also reported seeing UFOs, and one even had a "dogfight" with one. Professor Felix Zigel, of Moscow's Aviation Institute, said: "His name was Arkady Apraksin. He was flying a jet fighter when he encountered a cigar-shaped UFO. Radar had also spotted it, and he was ordered to force it to land, or open fire.

"Apraksin began his approach, but the mystery craft fired a fan-shaped beam which momentarily blinded him and killed his controls and the engine. He had to glide into a landing."

On June 14, 1980, another Soviet flier reported a UFO above Moscow that played cat-and-mouse with him. "Its manoeuvers were too bizarre for our jet to duplicate," said Professor Zigel. "Suddenly it took off at incredible speed." The pilot said the craft seemed almost 900 feet wide, and was circular.

Four months later, on October 22, Captain Vladimir Dubstov spotted a similar-size saucer hovering below him as he flew his patrol bomber over the Arctic Ocean. He changed course to circle it.

"He told me it was truly immense," said Professor Zigel. "A cone of light protruding down from it gave it an eerie appearance, but it showed no sign of life. Then Dubstov's instruments went haywire, and he lost altitude. The UFO took off vertically and soared past him, leaving behind a greenish-blue cloud. Dubstov nursed his crippled jet home and reported the incident."

Phantoms fight "cover up"

American airline pilots were furious in 1954 when the CIA and USAF imposed military-style curbs on them reporting UFOs. The clamp-down followed a conference in February when Military Air Transport Service Intelligence officers met the heads of major airlines to try to speed up the process of reporting UFOs spotted during civilian flights.

Until then, pilots had reported strange objects after they landed. Now the Air Force instructed them to radio the news to MATS HQ in Washington, or the nearest air base, while in flight. And it asked them not to discuss sightings, or give information to newspapers.

A month later, regulations threatening Air Force pilots with ten years jail and a fine of $10,000 for "failing to maintain absolute secrecy" were extended to cover civilian air crews. Understandably, the airline veterans reacted angrily. A protest petition was signed by 450 men, 50 of whom, all with at least 15 years service, said at a meeting that the censorship bid "bordered on the ridiculous." It was, they said, "a lesson in lying, intrigue, and the Big Brother attitude carried to the ultimate extreme."

The pilots knew that the curbs were part of a cover-up, for all had seen a UFO with their own eyes. Many had seen several. They revealed that five or ten sightings were reported every night by commercial pilots in America alone, and said that it was almost routine to warn passengers to put on seat belts when UFOs were near.

Some of the civilian sightings over the last 40 years have been every bit as spectacular as those reported by the air forces.

Early on July 23, 1948, Captain Clarence Chiles and his co-pilot John Whitted saw a craft from their Eastern Airlines DC-3 over Montgomery, Alabama. A cigar-like projectile was heading for the Dakota from the northeast.

Chiles swung his plane to the left, and as the UFO passed

Chichester and the UFO

Probably the first air-to-air sighting of a UFO was by Francis Chichester, later to earn fame as a round-the-world yachtsman. In 1931, he was piloting a tiny plane from Australia to New Zealand when a strange airship appeared, a dull grey-white colour with brightly flashing lights. The disc followed him for some miles across the Tasman Sea, occasionally vanishing behind clouds, before accelerating out of sight.

it 200 yards away, he noted two rows of portholes emitting an uncanny light along the side of the metallic, wingless shape. "There was a deep blue glow on the underside of the craft, and a 15-yard trail of orange-red flame," the pilot reported. The object stopped when it drew level with the plane, then shot upwards at great speed. The Dakota wobbled, as if caught in the blast. Chiles later found one passenger who had not been sleeping, and had seen the "great streak of light."

Six years later, the crew and passengers of the BOAC stratocruiser *Centaurius* watched an even better in-flight show. As the plane approached Goose Bay, Labrador, on June 29, 1954, en route from New York to Shannon and London, Captain James Howard noticed a large dark object emerge from clouds four miles to his left, apparently flying parallel with him. It was surrounded by six smaller blobs.

Howard radioed ahead to Goose Bay, and two US F80 Sabre jets scrambled. What happened next was seen by the 11 crew and 19 passengers of the stratocruiser, and described later by investigator John Carnell.

He wrote: "When 15 miles away, one of the fighter pilots radioed that he had the unknown objects and the airliner on his radar scope. At that instant the six smaller objects, which seemed like discs, moved into single file and appeared to enter the larger object, which then began to fade, disappearing as the fighter appeared overhead."

Carnell, who described the mother ship as "a large, shape-changing object, rather like a swarm of bees, but solid," said the same formation was seen several times that year, over both America and Europe.

Keeping tabs on Concorde

People living near London's Heathrow Airport claim to have seen UFOs keeping watch on the Anglo-French supersonic jet Concorde. Mrs. Dee Godden, 65, of Chiswick, West London, said she first saw one in August 1979.

"A huge reddish ball of light appeared in the sky right in Concorde's flightpath," she said. "I thought there was going to be an almighty crash, but when Concorde reached the spot, it just flew straight through it. The shape looked as if it was keeping watch on the plane."

Her husband Ernest, 64, also saw the light. "I was skeptical when my wife told me what she had seen," he recalled. "I looked out of the window of our flat, and saw a shimmering object. It stayed in the sky for about 17 minutes."

At Heathrow, officials said: "Nothing was picked up on

radar, so we cannot explain the sighting." But UFO researcher Barry Gooding said: "It is quite possible that UFOs from another planet are keeping watch on technological advances such as Concorde."

Unchartered activities

A dream trip to a sunshine island turned into a nightmare flight for 109 German and Austrian tourists when UFOs took too close an interest in their charter jet in November 1979. Captain Javier Lerdo-Tejeda, 34, a pilot with 15 years flying experience, was at the controls as the Caravelle took off at 9:30 A.M. from the Mediterranean isle of Majorca,

bound for the Canary Islands. But soon after levelling out, he noticed two very bright red lights in the sky.

"I was intrigued because they seemed to be flying in formation," said Captain Lerdo-Tejeda. "They were moving abreast at a slight angle to me, but getting closer all the time. They were about 15 miles away when we were at 23,000 feet, but only half a mile off when we reached 28,000 feet. Soon I realized they were almost on a collision course—they were virtually on top of me."

The pilot ordered his passengers and six crew to put their seat belts back on, and radioed ahead to Barcelona control tower. He was told there were no aircraft in his flight path, and nothing on the radar screens.

"I decided to call in help from the Spanish air force and the Madrid radar station," said Captain Lerdo-Tejeda. "The equipment there is more sensitive than that used for civilian

traffic, and they had picked up two objects which seemed to be very close to my plane.

"I swung my aircraft away sharply from the red lights and began descending at 5,000 feet a minute to 15,000 feet—an extremely steep dive for the passengers. Madrid was still monitoring the UFOs, and said the objects suddenly dropped 12,000 feet in just 30 seconds, following me. I know of no aircraft capable of doing that."

He continued to take evasive action, trying in vain to shake off the two shadows. Then, 30 miles out to sea off Valencia on Spain's south-west coast, an air force Mirage fighter arrived. The pilot instantly spotted the two glowing red shapes, apparently chasing the airliner. But seconds after the fighter jet zoomed into sight, the lights suddenly vanished.

A shaken Captain Lerdo-Tejeda swung back to Valencia for an unscheduled stop, and filed a full report of his dramatic encounter. "I have never known such danger, and I have been flying for nearly half my life," he told stunned officials. His crew backed his account in separate interviews.

Spain's Transport and Communications Minister, Sanchez Teran, was in Valencia at the time, and spoke to Captain Lerdo-Tejeda. He said later: "I am now prepared to believe that unidentified flying objects do exist."

They never returned

Have UFOs caused civilian planes to crash? In 1953, the pilot of a DC-6 airliner flying from Wake Island in the Pacific to Los Angeles reported UFOs approaching before his radio went dead. Searchers later found wreckage and 20 bodies. And over Michigan, as reported elsewhere in this book, witnesses saw a curious ball of light in the sky on the night a DC-4 crashed, killing 58 people.

On a Saturday evening in late October, 1978, Frederick Valentich vanished while flying his single-engined Cessna 182 from Melbourne, Australia, to King Island. He was near Cape Otway, 35 miles south of Melbourne over the Bass Strait, when he told air controllers he was being followed by an aircraft with four bright lights.

When officials asked if he could identify the plane, he radioed: "It's not an aircraft, it's . . ." The set went dead. Two minutes later it came alive briefly again, and Valentich said: "I'm orbiting and the thing is orbiting on top of me also . . . it has a green light and sort of metallic light on the offside." He added that his engine was choking and rough-idling, then all contact was lost.

Rescue planes and ships scoured the area but found nothing except an oil slick, thought to be too large to be caused by a light aircraft. Valentich's girlfriend, Rhonda Rushton, 16, said: "I know he is alive, and we will see him soon." She added that she had given government officials "top secret" information. A spokesman said: "We promised to keep details of the interview confidential."

Authors Kevin Killey and Gary Lester used the disappearance as evidence of their claim, in 1981, that the Bass Strait was another Bermuda Triangle. They said a new four-engine plane carrying a crew of two and ten passengers had vanished there in 1932, and in 1979 a racing sloop and her crew of five disappeared without trace. They renamed the waters between Melbourne and Tasmania the Devil's Meridian.

"Flying saucers, the size of battleships . . . "

Three UFOs were also spotted over the Iberian peninsula by the crew and 100 passengers of a British Airways Trident. Captain Denis Wood saw them as he flew to Faro, Portugal—and again as he made the return flight to London later the same day.

It happened over the Portuguese west coast on July 30, 1976. Captain Wood, 42, from Haslemere, Surrey, was told by air traffic controllers that an unidentified flying object had been reported in the area. He scanned the skies, and saw a bright object like nothing he had seen before in 20 years of flying. "It was not a satellite, weather balloon or a star," he said later.

As he invited the passengers to look at the UFO, two more objects appeared in the night sky. "They were cigar-shaped, and appeared to come from nowhere," said First Officer Colin Thomas, 38, from Camberley, Surrey. "They took up positions to the right and below the first object. It was just after 8 P.M., and I could see them clearly for eight minutes. They did not move." Thomas had served 12 years as an RAF fighter pilot, and had flown with British Airways for seven years, but he too had never seen anything like the UFOs.

After dropping the 100 holiday-makers at Faro, Captain Wood, Flight Officer Thomas and the third crewman, Stephen Sowerby, of Richmond on Thames, set out at once for home. As they flew through the area where they had seen the UFOs, Captain Wood switched on his radar scanner and tilted it towards the spot where the shapes had been. They were still there.

"The two cigar-shaped objects were exactly where they had been," said Captain Wood. "We got to within seven miles of them, then they just disappeared off the side of the screen."

The crew described the UFOs later as "flying saucers, the size of battleships." But it was ten months before they told the world about them. "We were afraid people would ridicule us," said one of them.

Some people did just that after they announced their sighting. The Science Research Council, in London, said the main "UFO" was probably a giant research balloon, on its way from Sicily to America. Rays of the setting sun would have caught the plastic fabric, making it appear brilliantly lit. And the secondary UFOs were probably either ballast being thrown overboard as the gas of the balloon cooled, or clouds of fine steel shot used to measure the wind.

Watchers on the Moon?

A top American space consultant claims that two UFOs were watching when Neil Armstrong took his "one small step for a man, one giant leap for mankind" by walking on the Moon's surface on July 20, 1969.

The astronaut spotted them on the rim of a nearby crater as he stepped out of his Apollo 11 spacecraft, according to Maurice Chatelain, who had left the National Aeronautics and Space Administration team by the time he made the claim in September, 1979.

While Armstrong was reporting his sighting to Houston control, Chatelain said, co-pilot Buzz Aldrin filmed the alien craft from inside Apollo.

But, alleged Chatelain, NASA ordered a cover-up of the incident. Mission controllers blacked out Armstrong's radio report from worldwide broadcasts of the historic event "for security reasons."

NASA dismissed the story as "absolutely ridiculous." Chief spokesman John McLeaish said: "The only breaks in transmission from Apollo 11 occurred when it was on the other side of the Moon. The only conversations we have never made public were private talks between the astronauts and doctors."

Chatelain's story received unexpected backing—from Moscow. Physicist Dr. Vladimir Azhazha said: "We heard about this episode two years ago. I am certain it took place, but it was censored by NASA."

Soviet space expert Professor Sergei Boshich added: "It is my opinion that beings from another civilization picked up radio signals from Earth and spied on the Apollo landing to learn the extent of our knowledge. Then they took off without making contact."

Other American astronauts have had close encounters with strange craft. In 1953, Gordon Cooper, later to join the NASA programme, saw a UFO while piloting a plane

Buzz Aldrin standing on the Moon, with Neil Armstrong and the Eagle landing craft reflected in his visor.

over Germany. He said: "I now firmly believe in extraterrestrial craft."

In 1965, James McDivitt and Ed White were orbiting Earth 100 miles up in Gemini 4 when they spotted a silver cyinder with protruding antennae. McDivitt started taking pictures of it, but then the two men had to prepare for evasive action as the UFO moved closer. Just when a collision seemed inevitable, the curious craft vanished.

Mission control at Houston dismissed the shape as one of Gemini's booster rockets, in orbit alongside the ship. But McDivitt said: "It was in the wrong place at the wrong time for that."

Eight years later, astronauts Jack Lousma, Owen Garriot and Alan Bean saw a rotating red shape from Skylab 2. They spent ten minutes photographing it, 270 miles above Earth. Again NASA denied that the shining capsule was another spacecraft.

Gordon Cooper said: "NASA and the Government know very well that intelligent beings from other planets regularly visit our world to enter into discreet contact and observe us.

"They have an enormous amount of evidence, but have kept quiet in order not to alarm people."

9

What Are They, Who Are They, and Why Are They Here?

The daunting dossier of UFO data over the years means that they can no longer be shrugged aside as mere pie in the sky. But once we accept that craft flown by some non-human intelligence may be invading our air space, there are disturbing questions to be answered. Where do they come from? Who controls them? And why are they here?

Do UFOs exist, or are they just a figment of man's imagination? If they are real, where do they come from? And why are they hovering over and landing on Earth?

UFOs have been reported by too many serious, sensible people to be merely dismissed by skeptics as hallucination, mass hysteria, a mystical yearning of the human psyche, or a rebellion against impersonal science. Millions all over the world report having seen them—15 million in the United States alone in 1973. At Dr. J. Allen Hynek's Illinois Centre For UFO Studies, more than 50,000 sightings are contained in a computerized data bank, all of them sightings that defy explanation.

UFO researchers admit that up to 90 per cent of reported UFOs turn out to be natural phenomena or freak conditions. The planet Venus, advertising planes, military and civilian aircraft, comets, meteors and falling stars, giant balloons, saucer-shaped lenticular cloud formation, ball lightning, even army flares and flights of migrating geese, have all been mistaken for spacecraft. But there always remain 10 to 20 per cent of sightings for which nobody can find a rational cause.

Cover-ups by governments have possibly prompted UFOlogists to make exaggerated claims on occasions. Anxious to prove that UFOs exist, they have often embroidered what was really seen, or ignored evidence conflicting with their version of the facts.

But today more and more governments admit the existence of objects in the sky which come from somewhere beyond human control. Despite America's policy of denying the possibility of UFOs, its armed forces have drawn up procedures to deal with them. In 1957, a CIA source admitted: "One thing is for sure, we're being observed from outer space." Russia, Italy, Brazil and Argentina, having issued official reports of sightings, unequivocally accept the existence of UFOs. And in 1974, French Defense Minister Robert Galley said: "There is a steady accumulation of sightings of luminous phenomena that are sometimes spherical, sometimes ovoid, and which are characterized by extraordinarily rapid movement.

"Reports from the gendarmerie, from pilots, from people who are heads of air establishments, and a lot of other material, are absolutely impressive . . . and disturbing. It is certain that there are things we do not understand and that are at present relatively inexplicable."

Even Britain does not deny the possibility of manned flights by non-humans, though it has always stuck closely to the cynical American public line. An RAF spokesman said: "The Ministry of Defence does not discount the possibility of intelligent life existing in other parts of the galaxy. However, we have yet to have irrefutable proof that such

---

The Greek cover-up

Eminent Greek scientist Paul Santorini stunned members of his country's astronautical society in February 1967 when he announced that there was "a world blanket of secrecy" about UFO activities—because the authorities did not want to admit the existence of forces against which Earth had "no possibility of defence."

Professor Santorini, then over 70 and the most respected scientist in Greece, revealed that in 1947 the Greek army had called him in to lead a team of engineers to investigate what were thought to be Russian missiles flying over the country.

"We soon established that they were not missiles," he said. "But before we could do any more, the army, after conferring with foreign officials, ordered the investigation stopped. Foreign scientists flew to Greece for secret talks with me."

Professor Santorini added that he had no doubt aliens were "visiting Earth to collect plant and animal specimens," but he would not guess why.

life exists. So far, no one has provided 100 per cent cast-iron evidence.''

In 1977, when the flood of UFO reports from the Broadhaven Triangle in Wales was at its peak, a Defence Ministry spokesman said: ''We accept that reports are made by sane, rational people, and that a hundred people do not imagine they saw something. But no physical evidence was found that anything had happened.

''We only investigate UFO reports to find whether there is a threat to our defences. If there is no threat, that is the end of the matter. We do not investigate whether UFOs exist, or what causes them.'' When asked who decided there was no danger to the nation's defences, the spokesman said: ''We are not prepared to discuss how we investigate.''

Private UFO researchers are more willing to discuss how they operate. Dr. Hynek, Stanton Friedman and Raymond E. Fowler in America, Norman Oliver, Jenny Randles and Stewart Campbell in Britain, all take detailed statements from witnesses, and check their background carefully with friends, relatives and employers, to make sure they are reliable people not given to hallucination or hoaxes. They then search painstakingly for possible alternative explanations, and often find them.

Over the years, patterns have emerged from those sightings that have survived rigorous scrutiny. UFOs are usually saucer-, cigar- or egg-shaped, often with illuminated domes and almost always with navigational or warning lights in patterns different from those used by Earth aircraft.

They seem to arrive over Earth in waves—1947, 1952, 1954, 1966–7, 1973 and 1975 were peak years for sightings in America; 1962 and 1977–8 in Russia; 1954, 1968, 1973 and 1977–9 in Britain; 1952–4, 1968 and 1973 in Western Europe; 1957, 1962 and 1965 in South America, particularly Brazil; 1959, 1965 and 1978–9 in Australasia and the Far East; and 1946 in Scandinavia, when thousands of mystery rockets were seen over Norway and Sweden.

UFOs seem able to defy all the laws of nature as we understand them—possibly the reason why many scientists deny their existence, preferring a world where all is rational and explicable. They move at a pace that would tear human

A judicial breakthrough

In September 1977, a Phoenix, Arizona UFO group filed a lawsuit against the CIA under the Freedom of Information Act. William Spaulding, director of Ground Saucer Watch Incorporated, alleged that the agency possessed thousands of documents about its involvement with UFOs, and had actively conspired to keep them secret from the public by denying their existence.

The case was backed by Citizens Against UFO Secrecy, a national body, and the CIA lost. A Washington judge ordered them to search their files for all UFO material. A total of 10,000 pages were found, but only 900 released, the rest being withheld on national security grounds. Nevertheless, Citizens Against UFO Secrecy hailed it as a victory. Even the admission that files existed was a breakthrough against the blanket of governmental obfuscation.

beings apart, and fly at supersonic speeds without sonic bangs. They change direction and height in ways that make gravity a joke, and produce high-tension electrical charges that not only turn them luminous, but disrupt Earth's power sources.

Many of them are manned by beings who seem to fall into roughly three categories—small creatures less than 4 feet tall with outsize heads and one-piece silver or green uniforms; man-size aliens with wide eyes and thin lips; and giants of about 7 feet. There is also a rare group of fur-covered or hairy beings, approximately 4 feet tall.

Where do they come from? The most popular theory is that they are visitors from another planet. UFOlogists noted that the sighting peak years of 1967 and 1973 coincided with the time when the orbit of Mars brought it closest to Earth; they wondered whether Martians had to wait for

"They are already here"

Many people in Spain believe that aliens from space are already living on Earth. For more than 30 years, a group who call themselves Ummo have been sending papers through the post and holding long late-night telephone conversations with people all over the country, alleging that they landed from a spacecraft in France in 1950 to help mankind reach maturity. They claim to come from the planet of Ummo which, they say, orbits the star known on Earth maps of the universe as Wolf 424.

All communications from Ummo have a thumbprint seal with a curious symbol, three horizontal lines crossing one vertical one. In May 1967, members of a Spanish space flight discussion group received invitations bearing the symbol. They were to gather on June 1 at a café in Santa Monica, near Madrid, for evidence of Ummo's existence.

They were there at the appointed time, and, sure enough, an object looking like a flying saucer arrived, the Ummo symbol on its underside. It performed aerial antics over the Madrid suburb of San José de Valderas before landing briefly in view of the café. Many witnesses took photographs of the strange craft before it flew away again. No one has since been able to trace Ummo to find out whether they really are aliens—or just very clever hoaxers.

suitable conditions to travel, just as Russia and America had to select exactly the right moments to launch their Venus probes.

The Dogons of Mali, incredibly, knew of the star Sirius centuries before human astronomers located it. Other UFO witnesses, too, have spoken of meeting beings who said they came from planets as yet undiscovered—planets from galaxies other than our Milky Way. Earthly science says this is impossible. It knows of nothing that travels faster than the speed of light, and scientists argue that it would take too long for extra-terrestrials to reach us, even if they thought the trip worth making.

Yet recent discoveries about telepathy open the door to new thinking about the possibility of teleportation. And it is not beyond human imagination to believe that, if beings of superior intelligence have developed flying saucers far more manoeuverable than anything we possess, they may also have come up with ways of journeying in suspended animation.

"These things are evil"

The Church frowns on the growing interest in unidentified flying objects. The Bishop of Norwich, one of two top clerics who attended the 1979 House of Lords debate on the subject, said: "I am very concerned. The mystery surrounding UFOs today is helping to build up a climate of credulity, and, in certain cases, even of superstition, with the danger of ersatz spirituality."

One clergyman, who has studied UFOs for 30 years and written a book about them, believes they are the work of the Devil, and have an evil influence on people. The Rev. Eric Inglesby said: "People expect UFOs to be benevolent beings. There is no proof whatsoever that this is the case. Quite the opposite.

"I have known many cases where people have been very disturbed, even to the point of a form of spirit possession which in many cases is undoubtedly evil. Some of the UFOs are frightfully dangerous. I even know of cases where people were so oppressed by sightings of UFOs that they had to be exorcised by a priest."

Three other schools of thought say UFO aliens come from Earth itself. Einstein first developed the theory that two worlds can coexist in different dimensions, that they intertwine, each invisible to the other for most of the time. Many UFOlogists believe that is what UFOs do, crossing over into our consciousness only when they want to, or when they can.

Others argue that interplanetary travellers settled on Earth long ago, adopting the language and customs of the countries where they landed. Ralph Blum, three times winner of top American Science Foundation awards, says experts have never satisfactorily explained why some people are more intelligent than others, or born leaders, and he believes that superbeings could be conducting experiments with human life. "Seriously, the person you are married to could be descended from beings from beyond Earth," he says.

Kenneth Huer, former astronomy lecturer at New York's Hayden Planetarium, says: "It is possible that aeons ago our ancestors came from outer space as whole beings in spaceships. Or they could be here in great numbers, but we are unconscious of their presence. They may be here in extraordinary unrecognizable forms."

Such a theory would explain the puzzling "men in black" reported by some UFO witnesses. The woman whose claim of being raped by an alien in Somerset, England, has been reported in this book. She later told UFO investigator Barry King she received letters and phone calls warning her not to talk about it; and two mysterious men visited her husband and herself several times to stress the desirability of secrecy.

The third idea is that UFOs originate from the centre of the Earth. Throughout the ages, some scientists have argued that the Earth is not solid, but hollow. Plato spoke of "tunnels both broad and narrow into the interior"; and Buddhist doctrine teaches of a subterranean world called Agharta, where millions live in a subtropical paradise ruled over by the King of the World, who relays messages to surface humans via monks who travel secret passages that possibly emerge in the Himalayas. Other academics have seriously suggested that survivors of Atlantis, even the fairies and

"They want to help us"

Psychic Greta Woodrew, of Connecticut, claimed she was contacted by aliens, and told that they are waiting to help Earth cope with future catastrophes.

She said she met beings from a planet called Ogatta, many light years away, during experiments at the Ossining, New York, laboratories of para-psychologist Dr. Andrija Puharich.

The first contact came in December, 1976. Mrs. Woodrew was put into a deep hypnotic trance. She claimed she found herself in a long shadowy tunnel being guarded by a man-like creature called Hshames and two bird-like "entities." Hshames stood just over five feet tall, and his skin was covered with minute feathers. He had large, gold-flecked, luminous, lashless eyes, and his upper lip resembled a beak. They conversed by telepathy, and the figure told her about Ogatta.

During the second experiment, Mrs. Woodrew claimed that her soul left her body, and she was transported to Ogatta itself. Everything shone, and the surface was covered with dots like glistening halves of marbles. They held a precious water-like substance.

At the next session, according to Mrs. Woodrew, an entity called Ogatta spoke to her. "He said beings had set up a way-station on the minor planet Vesta in our solar system, which will be used to help Earth. An armada of spacecraft, called gattae, would come down to Earth after drastic changes occurred. Their preparations were well under way."

Mrs. Woodrew claimed she was then shown scenes of devastation which could happen to Earth in the next few decades. Floods, hurricanes, super-magnetic storms, droughts, earthquakes, volcanic

> eruptions, tidal waves that covered entire cities, and people dying of thirst and hunger.
>
> "I was told by the extra-terrestrials that they were survivors of what could come," Mrs. Woodrow said. "Then they said, 'Despite what man can do to man and nature's plan, there are civilizations in the cosmos who believe planet Earth is worth helping.' "

goblins of world folklore, live below the Earth, far more advanced technologically than ourselves.

Late in the 19th century, Norwegian sailor Olaf Jansen claimed that he and his father had sailed into this wonderful underworld, and lived with the giants there for two years. He said the inhabitants lived for 500 years, had the power to propel machines by drawing energy from the air, and were well aware of what was happening to humans on the surface of Earth. Jansen's story was so ridiculed that he stopped telling it—but on his death bed, he repeated the details to an American journalist.

In the 20th century, Adolf Hitler launched massive searches for tunnels to an inner Earth. But the belief in a subterranean wonder-world really took off when Rear Admiral Richard Byrd flew 1,700 miles beyond the North Pole in 1947 and 2,300 miles beyond the South Pole in 1956. On both flights, he claimed to have come across iceless lands of mountains. lakes and green vegetation recorded on no maps.

Then, on November 23, 1968, pictures from the American satellite ESSA-7 showed the North Pole without its normal cloud cover—and revealed a perfectly round, dark circle. Advocates of the hollow Earth idea instantly claimed this to be the entry to the underworld. They said the world was not round, but indented top and bottom, so that the true Poles were in mid-air. This, they said, is why compasses go awry 150 miles from both the North and South Poles; and such holes, both in the Arctic and Antarctic, are where UFOs are supposed to emerge.

"Only when we believe"

Aliens will not reveal their mission on Earth until enough people accept the reality of UFOs, and man can understand them on a technical and scientific basis. That is the verdict of Dr. Harley Rutledge after a seven-year study of the subject.

He claims UFOs zip around the Earth constantly, reading our minds and listening to our conversations. But they usually travel so fast that we cannot see them. And they only appear when they want to attract our attention.

Dr. Rutledge, chairman of the physics department of the Southwestern Missouri State University, said he was a skeptic when the study began in 1973. He and nearly 500 helpers spent 2,000 hours studying the sky over three Missouri towns, Cape Giradeau, Piedmont and Farmington, and reported 157 sightings of 178 UFOs. In 16 cases observers noted UFO reaction to the team's movements, voices, radio signals and thoughts.

"We sensed that we were dealing with an intelligence," said Dr. Rutledge. "I felt as though something was toying with us. On one occasion we deliberately changed our viewing position and moved 10 miles to the west to get directly into the path of UFOs we had been observing. The UFOs changed direction to go round us, just as they had done before."

He added: "I suspect their game is gradually to create general acceptance by repeated appearances. More UFO flaps will occur from location to location, winning converts.

"When we understand them, and when most of the world's inhabitants accept the reality of UFOs, then we will meet them face to face and know why they are here."

Wherever they come from, what are UFOs up to? Why are they interested in Earth? Are they, as claimed by Douglas Adams, author of the *Hitch-hiker's Guide to the Galaxy*, simply rich young galactic playboys in interstellar sports cars who enjoy tantalizing Earth? Or have they a serious purpose?

Many people believe they may be beings from a planet that has become uninhabitable, who are looking for a new place to live. Others argue that they are worried about man destroying himself with toys such as nuclear power, which he can neither understand nor control responsibly.

Others see humanity as being in some sort of zoo, given regular medical checkups to see how it is developing, and even abducted occasionally for interbreeding to ensure that it improves over the ages.

The problem is, we can only judge the behavior of UFOs by our own standards. We may assume that the UFOnauts want to land, but are waiting until we are ready, or less aggressive towards them; perhaps they are holding back for fear of causing panic here, or triggering a breakdown of society once people realize that Earth has no defence against powerful forces seemingly able to invade its skies at will.

Lord Clancarty, who persuaded the British House of Lords to hold a debate on UFOs, says: "I believe that with our nuclear and pollution problems, there is concern for us coming from outer space. I think we are on the verge of an official landing on Earth." Others say the recent UFO sightings are merely reconnaissance flights heralding the Second Coming in 1999.

But perhaps the most realistic assessment comes from Dr. Stanton Friedman, who was an American government physicist before becoming a full-time UFOlogist. He says: "They are not interested in settling here, they are just worried about what we will do when we get out there."

Dr. Friedman, who says he has spoken to more than 90 former senior military officers about messages from UFOs picked up by tracking stations, adds: "They know it is only a matter of time—say about 100 years, nothing in galactic terms—before we send out starships and attempt to become part of the Galactic Federation. Before that happens they want to make sure they know everything about us.

"They see a primitive society which is mostly engaged in tribal warfare, so of course they want to know a lot more about us."

Jim Lorenzen, director of the Aerial Phenomena Research Organization, says: "For them to attempt to land here in any numbers would be just like us intruding on an ancient civilization deep in the jungle and imposing our civilization on them. The result would be destructive.

"In the end it is up to us. We now hold the key to a universe that we never thought existed. It is up to us whether we use that key—or perish in the insanity of war."

What should you do if you see a UFO? Researchers give these five guidelines:

1. Try to confirm the sighting by finding other witnesses.

2. If you have a camera, use it.

3. Compare the UFO with local landmarks. This can help establish its size and speed.

4. When you get home, draw the UFO immediately and write down what you saw.

5. Tell the police, RAF or a local UFO group.